Atlas of
Tongue
Diagnosis

Atlas of
Tongue
Diagnosis

Project Editor: Wang Li-zi
Copy Editor: Zhao Dan
Book & Cover Designer: Yin Yan
Typesetter: Wei Hong-bo

Atlas of Tongue Diagnosis

Ding Cheng-hua
Professor of Chinese Medicine,
Jiangxi University of TCM, Nanchang

Sun Xiao-gang
Professor of Technology,
Nanchang University, Nanchang

Edited by Andrea Elliott, M.S. TCM

人民卫生出版社
PMPH PEOPLE'S MEDICAL PUBLISHING HOUSE
BEIJING · LONDON · NEW YORK

Website: http://www.pmph.com
Book Title: Atlas of Tongue Diagnosis
中医舌诊图谱

Contact address: Bldg 3, 3 Qu, Fangqunyuan, Fangzhuang, Beijing 100078, P.R. China, phone/fax: 8610 6769 1034, E-mail: pmph@pmph.com

For text and trade sales, as well as review copy enquiries, please contact PMPH at pmphsales@gmail.com

First published: 2008
ISBN: 978-7-117-09960-8/R · 9961

Cataloguing in Publication Data:
A catalog record for this book is available from the CIP-Database China.
条形码

Printed in The People's Republic of China

ISBN 978-7-117-09960-8

9 787117 099608 >

Ding Cheng-hua

About The Authors

Professor Ding Cheng-hua was born in February 1957 and is a supervisor of graduate students and the dean of her department at Jiangxi University of Traditional Chinese Medicine.

She is an experienced teacher and the director of a course on Chinese medicine diagnostics, a quality course in Jiangxi province. Professor Ding Cheng-hua is also the member of several important committees, including the Committee on Chinese Medicine Diagnosis and the World Federation of Chinese Medicine Societies (WFCMS).

She graduated from Jiangxi University of Traditional Chinese Medicine in 1982 and currently teaches courses on Chinese medicine diagnosis and fundamental theories of Chinese medicine to undergraduate students, graduate students, and overseas students.

She has led or participated in more than ten national and ministerial or provincial research projects; and has published over twenty articles in many academic journals, such as the *Journal of Basic Medicine, Education of Chinese Medicine, Jiangxi Journal of Traditional Chinese Medicine, and the Journal of Jiangxi College of Traditional Chinese Medicine.*

In addition to the above achievements, Professor Ding Cheng-hua has assumed an active role in the compilation of over ten textbooks and monographs; she is the compiler of *Chinese Medicine Diagnosis* (a nationally-established textbook published by New Century), *Chinese Medicine Diagnosis – A Study Guide, Tongue Manifestation in Chinese Medicine* (Chinese-English edition), *Analysis of Syndrome Differentiation Methods in Chinese Medicine Diagnosis, Essentials of Fundamental Theories of Chinese Medicine, A Tutorial on the Experimental Use of Chinese Medicine,* and *Visceral Manifestations and Clinical Practice in Chinese Medicine.* Professor Ding has received many awards for her outstanding achievements in both research and education.

Sun Xiao-gang

About The Authors

Professor Sun Xiao-gang was born in February 1957 and is a supervisor of graduate students at Nanchang University. He is the chief English translator and reviser of this book.

He graduated from Jiangxi College of Engineering in 1982 and currently lectures undergraduate students and graduate students on such subjects as composite technology, nano science and technology, and English newspaper reading.

He has led or participated in more than ten national and ministerial or provincial research projects. Furthermore, he has published over twenty articles in numerous academic journals, such as *World Nonferrous Metals*, *Materials Review*, *New Carbon Materials*, and *Journal of Jiangxi College of Tradtional Chinese Medicine*. Professor Sun is also one of the chief compilers of this book.

In addition, Professor Sun has received many awards for his outstanding achievements in research and education.

Atlas of
Tongue
Diagnosis

EDITORIAL BOARD

Atlas of
Tongue
Diagnosis

Zhang Hui
(experimenter in education with electrical audio-visual aids at the Jiangxi University of Traditional Chinese Medicine, photographer and image processor)

Hu Ke
(director of the Jiangxi University of Traditional Chinese Medicine, data collector)

Chen Yao-hui
(attending physician at the People's Hospital of Jiangxi Province, data collector and arranger)

Zhou Zhi-gang
(lecturer at the Jiangxi University of Traditional Chinese Medicine, data collector)

Guo Hong-fei
(director doctor of Jiangxi University of Traditional Chinese Medicine, data collector)

Tang Xi-men
(professor of Jiangxi University of Traditional Chinese Medicine, data collection)

Cao Xiao-rui
(graduate student of Jiangxi University of Traditional Chinese Medicine, data collector and arranger)

Zhang Wen-chun
(professor of Jiangxi University of Traditional Chinese Medicine, data collector and arranger)

Chen Hai-bo
(lecturer of Jiangxi University of Traditional Chinese Medicine, image processor)

Zhao Dan
(diagnosis master of Beijing University of Traditional Chinese Medicine, translator)

Atlas of
Tongue
Diagnosis

PREFACE

Tongue diagnosis is a unique examination technique utilized in Chinese medicine. It is an essential component of clinical diagnosis. Many famous physicians in ancient as well as modern society have been proficient at tongue diagnosis.

The features and advantages of diagnostic methods in Chinese medicine include the ability to obtain information about pathology without causing any injury to the body. Clinical examination consists of inferring the state of the interior by looking at the exterior. Chinese medicine considers the body of a person to be an inseparable whole, and the tongue is like a mirror that reflects both the physiological functions and the pathological changes in the body. Because the tongue is closely related to the *zang-fu* organs, qi, blood, and body fluids, it can also express excess and deficiency of the *zang-fu* organs, exuberance and decline of the qi and blood, gain and loss of the fluids, the presence or absence of stomach qi, the nature of pathogenic evil, and the depth and location of disease.

Guided by theories of Chinese medicine, this book fully absorbs the essentials of many treatises on tongue diagnosis and extracts information from all relevant Chinese medicine textbooks and reference books of higher learning. It not only inherits the traditional style of the tongue exam, but also introduces the latest achievements of modern scientific research in Chinese medicine regarding tongue diagnosis. Pictures are accompanied by text with explanations in English, full and accurate information, concise wording, and clear images. This is all provided in a clear and comprehensible manner utilizing scientific data where applicable. Therefore, it not only targets a wide range of readers, but also supplies many valuable sources of information on tongue diagnosis to the world.

This book is comprised of an introduction followed by four chapters. The introduction discusses the origin and development of tongue diagnosis as well as important treatises on the subject. The first chapter covers abstract information on tongue diagnosis. The second chapter discusses observation of the tongue quality. The third chapter discusses observation of the tongue coating. The final chapter discusses the clinical significance and applications of tongue diagnosis. A product of professional photography utilizing sophisticated equipment, over 200 pictures make the abstract theories of tongue diagnosis more concrete and visible. This addition helps the readers

Atlas of
Tongue
Diagnosis

to understand the theories, master the procedures, and set a series of standards for tongue diagnosis. It also promotes the standardization of tongue diagnosis.

Although there is much information about tongue diagnosis and changes in the appearance of the tongue are complex, it is important not to neglect to evaluate changes in the nature of the tongue in terms of its vitality, shape, and the quality and color of the coating. If the essentials of tongue diagnosis are understood and the information is applied flexibly, then information about the physiology and pathology of the human body can be seized in a timely manner, resulting in an accurate diagnosis.

This book is suitable for:

- undergraduates, graduate students, and foreign students pursing a specialty in Chinese medicine.

- medical doctors who practice Chinese medicine or those who intend to combine the practice of Chinese medicine with Western integrative medicine in a clinical environment.

- people interested in Chinese medicine or self-taught individuals who are enthusiastic about staying healthy.

In addition, this book can be used as a standard reference for tongue diagnosis in the clinic, the classroom, or research; and utilized as a reference book for specialists in Chinese medicine and pharmacology.

We would like to express our profound thanks to the Health Department of Jiangxi Province for their great assistance in the publication of this book.

The Compiler
December 12th, 2007

Atlas of
Tongue
Diagnosis

TABLE OF CONTENTS

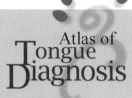

Atlas of
Tongue
Diagnosis

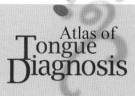

INTRODUCTION

Tongue diagnosis is the examination of changes in the tongue body and coating, and thereby serves as a method of diagnosing disease. Tongue diagnosis has a long history. The earliest accounts of examining the tongue to diagnose disease can be found in the *Yellow Emperor's Inner Classic* (*Huáng Dì Nèi Jīng*, 黄帝内经). Through research into the theory and clinical application of tongue diagnosis, each successive generation of physicians has continued to develop and perfect the theoretical systems and diagnostic methods that apply to tongue diagnosis.

THE ORIGINS OF TONGUE DIAGNOSIS

Tongue diagnosis has a long history in Chinese medicine. It was recorded in *Shang* Dynasty (1600-1046 B.C.) oracle bone inscriptions that *"the tongue foretells diseases"* (*zhēn jí shé*, 贞疾舌). "贞" means to practice divination or to be effective. This is the earliest recorded instance of tongue diagnosis or examination of the tongue.

During the Warring States period (475-221 B.C.), the famous physician Bian Que (扁鹊, Qin Yue-ren) used a variety of methods including palpation, observation, auscultation and inquiry to diagnose disease. The substance of Bian Que's tongue diagnosis was recorded in the *Pulse Classic* (*Mài Jīng*, 脉经) within which appears his four principles of tongue diagnosis. For instance, Bian Que states in his keys to diagnosing all reversal death pulses as recorded in the *Pulse Classic* that *"in the case of hemiplegia, if there is no loss of voice and the tongue can turn, the patient can be cured"*. This is regarding hemiplegia where the person cannot speak but can move the tongue. It represents a mild case that is relatively easy to cure. The diagnosis and prognosis for post stroke hemiplegia depends on the degree of movement and flexibility of the tongue body. Although only four items comprise Bian Que's comments on tongue diagnosis, his discussion is incisive and has become the foundation for future generations.

Tongue diagnosis already occupied an important role during the Warring States period when the *Yellow Emperor's Internal Classic* (*Huáng Dì Nèi Jīng*, 黄帝内经) was written. It is thought of as the first compilation of medical knowledge in ancient China. The *Yellow Emperor's Internal Classic* contained statements about dissection of the tongue, its function and relationship with the internal organs and channels as well as the clinical application of tongue diagnosis. The *Spiritual Pivot-Channels* (*Líng Shū-Jīng Mài*, 灵枢·经脉) states that "*The lips and the tongue are the root of the muscle tissue. If the pulse is not thriving then the muscles will become soft. If the muscles become soft then the tongue will become limp.*" This demonstrates that the tongue body is an organ composed mainly of muscle tissue that receives nourishment from the blood vessels. Without this nourishment the tongue will become limp, soft and unable to be used. The *Spiritual Pivot* also states that "*The tongue is the official of the heart*". Variations in the function and shape of the tongue reflect not only heart pathology, but also pathological changes in the other *zang-fu* organs. The *Spiritual Pivot* states that the channels of the five-*zang* and six-*fu* organs are linked directly or indirectly to the tongue. The channels of the *zang-fu* organs all pass through the tongue. Pathological changes in *zang-fu* organs function, or in the qi, blood and body fluids are necessarily reflected in the tongue. For this reason, it is possible to diagnose pathological changes in the *zang-fu* organs, qi, blood and body fluids based on an examination of the shape, color and moisture of the tongue, and the taste in the mouth.

From the publication of the *Yellow Emperor's Inner Classic* on, skilled physicians ceaselessly explored and gradually perfected the theory of tongue diagnosis. Zhang Zhong-jing (张仲景), the famous Eastern *Han* Dynasty (25-220 AD) physician, recorded more than twenty items regarding tongue diagnosis and proposed the term "tongue coating" in his work *Treatise on Cold Damage and Miscellaneous Diseases* (*Shāng Hán Zá Bìng Lùn*, 伤寒杂病论). Zhang Shi-wan (张石顽) explained in *Introduction to Cold Damage* (*Shāng Hán Xù Lùn*, 伤寒绪论) that "*The term tongue coating (tāi, 苔), originated in Zhang Zhong-jing. Since*

pathogenic evil progresses inward as do all things which are contained, it is called an embryo (tāi, 胎)". Later physicians referred to the fur-like material on the tongue as the "tongue coating," (*shé tāi*, 舌苔), a term which continues to be used today. The passage *"interior evil resides in the zang, the tongue is difficult to discuss"* established tongue diagnosis as one of the foundations for treatment based on pattern differentiation (*biàn zhèng lùn zhì*, 辨证论治). Though Wang Shu-he (王叔和), the famous *Jin* Dynasty (265-420 AD) physician, was known as a specialist in pulse diagnosis, there is no lack of cases where tongue diagnosis assists pulse diagnosis in his book. This shows that the practice of tongue diagnosis discussed in the *Treatise on Cold Damage and Miscellaneous Diseases* was already developed and well integrated as a method of diagnosing disease by the *Jin* Dynasty.

During the *Sui* Dynasty (581-618 AD), Chao Yuan-fang (巢元方) proposed a variety of appearances the tongue could exhibit and their clinical significance in the *General Treatise on the Causes and Symptoms of Diseases* (*Zhū Bìng Yuán Hòu Lùn*, 诸病源候论). He included stiffness, contraction, swelling, protrusion, dryness, ulceration, heaviness, and tongue sores, as well as descriptions of tongue coatings and color (yellow, white, yellow-white, burnt black, red, blue, dark red, slippery). Since the writing of the *Treatise on Cold Damage and Miscellaneous Diseases*, great strides have been made in the research and use of tongue diagnosis.

"Discussion of the Tongue" from the fourteenth volume of *Prescriptions Worth a Thousand Ounces of Gold* (*Qiān Jīn Fāng*, 千金方) compiled by Sun Si-miao (孙思邈) during the *Tang* Dynasty (618-907 AD) was the first Chinese medical treatise on tongue diagnosis. During the *Jin* and *Song* Dynasties, *Books on Surviving Patients* (*Huó Rén Shū*, 活人书) differentiated deficiency and excess of yin and yang on the basis of lack of dryness of the tongue and mouth. The *Key to Therapeutics of Children's Diseases* (*Xiǎo Ér Yào Zhèng Zhí Jué*, 小儿药证直诀) proposed the terms "protruding tongue" and "wagging tongue". The references to tongue diagnosis mentioned in the above literature are abundant but scattered. They

constitute the study of tongue diagnosis in embryonic form and cannot be considered treatises on tongue diagnosis.

Ao's *Golden Mirror Collection* (*Jīn Jìng Lù*, 金镜录), written during the *Yuan* Dynasty (1271-1368AD), summarized 12 pictures of the tongue and as such constitutes the earliest treatise on tongue diagnosis. Du Qing-bi (杜清碧), a contemporary of Ao, added 36 more tongue pictures and perfected the book by including therapeutic principles and formulas. It was called *Ao's Golden Mirror Collection of Cold Pathogenic Disease* (*Áo Shì Shāng Hán Jīn Jìng Lù*, 敖氏伤寒金镜录) by later generations and became the first work to break into tongue diagnosis. The *Golden Mirror Collection* says that diagnosing the tongue allows the physician to "*miraculously distinguish between life and death*". The pictures and accompanying text were compiled in two different forms as a continuation of the information presented in the *Yellow Emperor's Inner Classic*, the *Discussion of Cold Damage*, the *General Treatise on the Causes and Symptoms of Diseases*, and *Prescriptions Worth a Thousand Ounces of Gold*. It was the culmination of the greatest achievements in tongue diagnosis during the *Yuan* Dynasty and was regarded as a masterpiece. The unique inferences regarding the development and standardization of the evaluation of the tongue and its coating are still used to the present day.

During the *Ming* (1368-1644AD) and *Qing* (1644-1911AD) dynasties, researchers shed more light on the subject of tongue diagnosis. The practice reached a new stage of development during that time period. Treatises on tongue diagnosis emerged in large numbers, and they were very practical. The warm disease school of the *Ming* and *Qing* dynasties made many explorations of pattern identification based on diagnosis of the tongue. Physicians such as Wu You-ke (吴又可), Ye Tian-shi (叶天士), Xue Xue (薛雪), Wu Tang (吴塘), Wang Meng-ying (王孟英) and many others emphasized the important role of tongue diagnosis in diagnosing warm disease. Each of these famous physicians enriched the theory of tongue diagnosis as it related to warm disease pattern identification in their individual works.

After the founding of the People's Republic of China, research in tongue diagnosis entered a new period of rapid development. This led to the rearrangement and publication of many ancient medical works on tongue diagnoses that are of great clinical and practical value. Modern researchers have made use of modern scientific methods to research tongue diagnosis. Tongue diagnosis is widely applied in the clinical diagnosis and treatments of disease while there have been many gratifying achievements in research. This has enriched the theory of tongue diagnosis and raised its practical clinical significance in diagnosing disease.

BRIEF INTRODUCTION TO ANCIENT AND MODERN WORKS ON TONGUE DIAGNOSIS

1. *Ao's Golden Mirror of Cold Pathogenic Disease*, also known as *Tongue Diagnosis of Cold Pathogenic Disease*, was compiled in 1341 and published by the Shanghai Jin Zhang Publishing House. The original work had only 12 illustrative plates of tongue coatings. Du Qing-bi later arranged this volume according to his clinical experiences and perfected it by adding 24 new pictures for a total of 36 which were followed by treatment principles and herbal formulas. This work was the first treatise on tongue diagnosis to be researched and rearranged. *Ao's Golden Mirror of Cold Pathogenic Disease* marked the emergence of tongue diagnosis as a special topic of research in the *Yuan* Dynasty thereby propelling it to a new level of development.

2. *Methods of Tongue Observation in Cold Pathogenic Disease* (*Shāng Hán Guān Shé Xīn Fǎ*, 伤寒观舌心法) was written by Shen Dou-yuan (申斗垣) during the *Ming* Dynasty. This book deduced 137 types of tongues on the basis of the 36 tongues found in *Ao's Golden Mirror of Cold Pathogenic Disease*. Its contents are abundant and the statements insightful. It is a summary of Shen's many years of

clinical experience, and was the greatest work on tongue diagnosis at the time and a famous work during that era.

3. *Differentiation of the Tongue in Cold Pathogenic Disease* (*Shāng Hán Shé Jiàn*, 伤寒舌鉴) was written by Zhang Deng (张登) in 1668. This work took the essence of *Methods of Tongue Observation*, corrected the mistakes, and made it more precise. This book prepared a list of methods of observing the tongue dividing tongue coatings into eight different types including white, black, yellow, gray, red, purple, dark reddish brown and blue. It included 120 pictures of tongue coatings in all. Also attached was an appendix on the cold pathogenic tongue in pregnant women. The pictures were accompanied by explanations and identification of the patterns that were brief and to the point. This book divided tongue observation into coating and texture elaborating on the new experience of observing the tongue.

4. In 1764, Xu Ling-tai (徐灵胎) wrote the *Introduction to Tongue Differentiation* (*Shé Jiàn Zǒng Lùn*, 舌鉴总论), and most of the information was derived from Zhang Deng's *Differentiation of the Tongue in Cold Pathogenic Diseases*. Though Xu's clinical experience was limited, the book's conclusions regarding white, yellow, black, red, purple and blue tongues were precise and accurate, and constituted its saving grace.

5. Wang Wen-xuan (王文选) excerpted from *Differentiation of the Tongue in Cold Pathogenic Diseases* in 1838 and compiled parts of *The Experience of Surviving Patients* (1902). This book summarized the 36 tongue pictures in Du Qing-bi's work, the 120 tongue pictures in Zhang Deng's work and the 13 tongue pictures in Duan Zheng-yi's *Treatise on Acute Epidemic Febrile Diseases*. He selected 149 tongue pictures to be included in his book. This work was a great supplement to previous experience in tongue differentiation in warm disease. It is also a summary of tongue diagnosis before the *Qing* Dynasty.

6. *General Records of Tongue Coating* (*Shé Tāi Tǒng Zhì*, 舌胎统志), written by

Fu Song-yuan (傅松元) in 1874, reclassified the divisions of tongue coating color used by ancient doctors in addition to classifying the colors of the tongue body. This work divides tongue color into eight shades: withering white, pale, light red, red, crimson, purplish, blue and black. The information contained within it is abundant, and numerous clinical experiences are discussed. Especially notable are its precise and accurate descriptions of pathogenic tongues. What is called a pale tongue was created by Fu in this book, and it is different from a light red tongue.

7. *Correct Differentiation of the Tongue* (*Shé Jiàn Biàn Zhèng*, 舌鉴辨正), written by Liang Yu-yu (梁玉瑜) in 1894, originated from the *Differentiation of the Tongue* written by Wang Wen-xuan. It corrected the mistakes and added the differentiation of syndrome by observing the tongue for miscellaneous diseases. Liang emphasized observing the tongue according to channel syndrome differentiation and attached importance to "examining the coating by scraping the tongue". The author not only differentiated diseases due to externally contracted evil but also miscellaneous diseases. This book constitutes a great contribution to tongue diagnosis in China because the author dared to correct errors and seek truth from facts.

8. In 1911, Liu Heng-rui (刘恒瑞) wrote *New Method of Syndrome Differentiation by Observing the Tongue* (*Chá Shé Biàn Zhèng Xīn Fǎ*, 察舌辨证新法) and combined the traditional experience of tongue differentiation with modern medical knowledge. This book mainly discusses how to examine three kinds of tongue coatings (white, yellow and black). This involves differentiating changes in the tongue, making a prognosis, and distinguishing the waxing and waning and the false or true nature of the tongue coating. All of the author's ideas mentioned above were creative. This work was written precisely and simply, and serves as a helpful guide in the clinic due to its combination of the integration of theory and practice with diagnosis according to therapeutic principles.

9. In 1917, Cao Bing-zhang (曹炳章) wrote *Guide to Differentiating the Tongue*

(*Biàn Shé Zhǐ Nán*, 辨舌指南). He completed this book by using his consummate medical skills and versatile talent to collect 156 medical books from ancient to modern times in addition to more than 30 recently translated medical books plus various newspapers and magazines. This book included all methods of tongue differentiation and treatment of disease, discarding the dross and selecting the essential. This famous encyclopedia includes 122 color and 6 black and white pictures of the tongue. Its contribution was to sum up all the experiences of ancient doctors in one book while applying knowledge from the modern disciplines of anatomy, histology and physiology to explain the mechanism of tongue diagnosis. For example, he included information on the anatomy of the tongue body and microstructures (lingual papillae, taste buds, vessels and nerves). This work is abundant in content and famous for its research and success in summing up great achievements in the field of tongue diagnosis prior to the *Qing* Dynasty.

10. *Methods of Examining the Tongue for Clinical Practice* (*Lín Zhèng Yàn Shé Fǎ*, 临症验舌法) is divided into two volumes and was written by Yang Yun-feng (杨云峰) in 1923. The first volume introduced the analysis of pathogenic conditions of excess and deficiency of yin and yang by the quality and color of the tongue and coating, differentiated *zang-fu* organs conditions by examining the tongue, listed the main formula for every tongue picture and related it to therapeutic principles. The second volume introduced the indications and use of each formula. *Differentiation of the Tongue According to Zang-Fu Organs, Differentiation of the Tongue According to Excess and Deficiency, Differentiation of the Tongue According to Yin and Yang,* all proposed by Yang, served as important references for later researchers. The author intended to make tongue diagnosis precise and appropriate, and therefore could not expound in detail or engage in a broad and profound explanation of tongue diagnosis. This work is therefore a simple book on tongue diagnosis.

11. *Study of Chinese Tongue Diagnosis* (*Guó Yī Shé Zhěn Xué*, 国医舌诊学) was written by Qiu Jun-sheng (邱骏声) in 1933. This eye-catching book systematically arranged relevant documents on tongue diagnosis and included abundant content and knowledge gained from experience. The author explained statements in detail. This book was divided into three volumes. The first volume elaborated on the definition, history, scope and value of tongue diagnosis, characterized the physiological structure and functions of the tongue body, and outlined the correspondence of particular areas on the tongue to *zang-fu* organs; the second volume described coating color and texture, tongue color and body, a method of differentiation based on taste and feeling in the mouth, and tongue diagnosis of special conditions; the third volume was a pictoral explanation of tongue diagnosis that provided pattern differentiation and treatments for 145 different tongue pictures.

12. *Tongue Diagnosis in Traditional Chinese Medicine* (*Zhōng Yī Shé Zhěn*, 中医舌诊) published by the People's Medical Publishing House in 1960, was compiled by the basic Chinese medicine theory teaching and research group of the Chinese medicine department at the Beijing Institute of TCM. This was the first treatise on tongue diagnosis to be published after the founding of the People's Republic of China. It not only briefly introduced the history of tongue diagnosis, the structure of the tongue and its relationship to the *zang-fu* organs, the clinical significance of tongue diagnosis, methods of examining the tongue coating and tongue quality, but also described the kinds of tongue qualities that are associated with particular indications and therapeutic principles often seen in clinical practice. The authors inherited the essence of tongue diagnosis and made great progress in its development. This book was concise and explained the profound in simple terms. Its contents were broad but not mixed and disorderly, so it was an excellent reference book as well as a profound influence on later research and teaching.

13. *Research on Tongue Diagnosis* (*Shé Zhěn Yán Jiū*, 舌诊研究), published by the

Shanghai Scientific Technology Publishing House in 1965, was compiled by Chen Ze-lin (陈泽霖) and Chen Mei-fang (陈梅芳), and republished in 1982 after being revised. It was a treatise on tongue diagnosis that combined Chinese medicine with western medicine. The authors applied knowledge from the modern disciplines of anatomy, histology, embryology, biology, chemistry, physiology, pathology and pathophysiology to research on tongue diagnosis. They gained a thorough understanding of tongue diagnosis through mastery of all relevant material via the method of combining Chinese medicine with western medicine. This book narrated the general progression of developments, described the clinical significance and methods of tongue observation, elaborated on the many kinds of research methods that could be applied to tongue diagnosis, attached clinical cases to normal and pathogenic tongue pictures, and analyzed relevant factors in the formation of tongue diagnosis. In addition, they proposed their own creative ideas and and drew conclusions about clinical differentiation for every pathological tongue which could be used as a guide to differentiation in tongue diagnosis.

14. *TCM Atlas of Tongue Coating* (*Zhōng Yī Shé Tāi Tú Pǔ*, 中医舌苔图谱), published by the People's Medical Publishing House in September 1984, was compiled by Song Tian-bin (宋天彬). This book contained 257 color photos of tongues, more than previous books. The author emphasized the introduction of the principles of tongue diagnosis, their clinical significance, the relationship between tongue quality and tongue coating, methods of and cautions in tongue diagnosis, and the five parts of tongue diagnosis. The atlas was divided into seven parts: the normal tongue, the pale tongue, the light red tongue, the red tongue, the crimson tongue, the bluish purple tongue and others. This work was therefore a book of directly observed images which stressed single factor clinical significance.

15. *Inspecting the Tongue to Diagnose Disease* (*Wàng Shé Zhěn Bìng*, 望舌诊病), published by the Heilongjiang Scientific Technology Publishing House in March 1987, was written by Li Nai-min (李乃民). The distinguishing characteristic of this

book is that on the basis of a Chinese medical inspection and differentiation of the tongue, it combined modern medical methods and clinical experience. It was the first to combine observation of the tongue with modern medical diagnosis of a single disease as a method of diagnosing disease based on tongue diagnosis. The author summarized indications in the appearance of the tongue for 24 kinds of diseases in internal medicine, surgery and gynecology. For the first time in any treatise on tongue diagnosis, it made the appearance of the tongue a diagnostic standard for particular diseases.

16. *Atlas of Clinical Tongue Diagnosis and Treatment of Disease* (*Lín Chuáng Shé Zhěn Tú Pǔ Yǔ Jí Bìng Zhì Liáo*, 临床舌诊图谱与疾病治疗), published by the Academy Publishing House in January 1997, was compiled by Weng Wei-liang (翁维良). This book took the origin and development of tongue diagonosis from historical treatises and synthesized modern research on the subject. It included 120 color photos of pathological tongues with attached analysis of cases and put forward syndrome differentiation and treatment along with therapeutic formulas.

17. *Foundation and Clinical Research on Diagnosis of Sublingual Vessels* (*Shé Xià Luò Mài Zhěn Fǎ De Jī Chǔ Yǔ Lín Chuáng Yán Jiū*, 舌下络脉诊法的基础与临床研究), published by the Guangdong Science and Technology Publishing House in March 1998, was compiled by Jin Shi-ying (靳士英). This work first stated the origin, evolution and traditional theory of sublingual tongue diagnosis, then introduced the results of clinically applied observation and included 200 photos. This work filled a gap within tongue atlases on the diagnosis of sublingual vessels.

18. *Origins of Differentiation in Tongue Diagnosis* (*Shé Zhěn Yuán Jiàn*, 舌诊源鉴), published by the People's Medical Publishing House, was compiled by Wang Ji-li (王季藜). The particulars of this book are based on historical treatises on tongue diagnosis and include the essence of historical medical book descriptions of tongue diagnosis. It applied integrated Chinese and western medical theory and

includes a summary of combined practical experience from teaching, practice and research. This book systematically introduced the disease mechanisms of particular appearances of the tongue along with diagnostic and treatment methods. It is a treatise on the study of Chinese and western tongue diagnosis.

In addition, some medical works, although not treatises on tongue diagnosis, contained chapters or sections on the subject. Moreover, they developd the topic quite fully and are considered to be excellent works. For example, there is the section containing the four diagnostics in *Basics of Medicine* (*Yī Xué Rù Mén*, 医学入门) by Li Ting (李梴, 1575), the section on tongue diagnosis in *Criteria for Patterns and Treatment* (*Zhèng Zhì Zhǔn Shéng*, 证治准绳) by Wang Ken-tang (王肯堂, 1597), *Jing-yue's Complete Works-Differentiation of Tongue Color* (*Jǐng Yuè Quán Shū-Shé Sè Biàn*, 景岳全书·舌色辨) by Zhang Jie-bin (张介宾, 1624), *Secret Records from the Stone Chamber-Secret Methods for Differentiating the Tongue in Cold Damage* (*Shí Shì Mì Lù-Shāng Hán Biàn Shé Mì Fǎ*, 石室秘录·伤寒辨舌秘法) by Chen Shi-duo (陈士铎, 1687), the section on tongue diagnosis in *Concise Assessment of the Four Methods of Diagnosis* (*Sì Zhěn Jué Wēi*, 四诊抉微) by Lin Zhi-han (林之翰, 1723), *Introduction to Cold Damage-Differentiation of the Tongue* (*Shāng Hán Xù Lùn-Biàn Shé*, 伤寒绪论·辨舌) by Zhang Shi-wan (张石顽, 1795), *Guide to Cold Damage-Songs for Inspecting the Tongue and Differentiating the Pattern* (*Shāng Hán Zhǐ Zhǎng-Chá Shé Biàn Zhèng Gē*, 伤寒指掌·察舌辨症歌) by Wu Kun-an (吴坤安, 1776), *Bi-hua's Medical Mirror-Observing Tongue Color* (*Bǐ Huā Yī Jìng-Wàng Shé Sè*, 笔花医镜·望舌色) by Jiang Bi-hua (江笔花, 1824), *Warnings in Medicine-Differentiating Tongue Coating* (*Yī Mén Bàng Hè-Biàn Shé Tāi*, 医门棒喝·辨舌苔) by Zhang Nan (章楠, 1825), *Adhering to the Classics in Observation and Diagnosis-Outline of Diagnostic Methods for Observing the Tongue* (*Wàng Zhěn Dào Jīng-Wàng Shé Zhěn Fǎ Tí Gāng*, 望诊道经·望舌诊法提纲) by Wang Hong (汪宏, 1875), *Zhou's Medical Series-Differentiation of Tongue Texture and Coating* (*Zhōu Shì Yī Xué Cóng Shū-Shé Zhì Shé Tāi Biàn*, 周氏医学丛书·舌质舌苔辨) by Zhou Xue-hai

(周学海, 1894) and others. These works contain many incisive opinions and much valuable experience regarding tongue diagnosis. Aside from this, in the process of establishing the warm disease school, experience in the "warm disease inspection of the tongue" was firmly established and made abundant. For example, *Discussion of Warm Epidemics* (*Wēn Yì Lùn*, 温疫论) by Wu You-xing (吴有性, 1624), *Discussion of Warm-Heat Pathogen Disorders* (*Wēn Rè Lùn*, 温热论) by Ye Tian-shi (叶天士, 1746), *Discussion of Damp Heat* (*Shī Rè Lùn*, 湿热论) by Xue Xue (薛雪, 1754), *A View of Epidemic Rashes* (*Yì Zhěn Yī Dé*, 疫疹一得) by Yu Lin (余霖, 1794), *Externally Contracted Warm Diseases* (*Wài Gǎn Wēn Bìng Piān*, 外感温病篇) by Chen Ping-bo (陈平伯, 1824), *Treatises on the Differentiation and Treatment of Warm Diseases* (*Wēn Bìng Tiáo Biàn*, 温病条辨) by Wu Tang (吴瑭, 1798), *The Warp and Woof of Warm-Heat Pathogen Disorders* (*Wēn Rè Jīng Wěi*, 温热经纬) by Wang Meng-ying (王孟英, 1852) and others. They all enriched, supplemented and perfected theories of warm disease, and established a method of inspecting the tongue that was applicable to all warm-heat diseases. They combined tongue diagnosis with four level (*wei*-defense, qi, *ying*-nutrient, *xue*-blood) and triple burner pattern differentiation, and thereby established the principles for warm disease inspection of the tongue, pattern differentiation and treatment.

CHAPTER ONE

Fundamentals of Tongue Diagnosis

Section 1
Principles of Tongue Diagnosis

MORPHOLOGICAL STRUCTURE AND PHYSIOLOGICAL FUNCTIONS OF THE TONGUE

1. Morphological Structure

The tongue is the most important organ in the oral cavity. It is flat and long, and attached by muscles to the lower jawbone and the hyoid bone. It is a muscular organ composed of a mucus membrane and striated muscle. For this reason, the *Spiritual Pivot-Channels (Líng Shū-Jīng Mài, 灵枢·经脉)* says, *"muscle is the root of the lips and tongue"*.

The external form of the tongue includes the upper side called the tongue back and the underside called the tongue bottom. The tongue back is divided into two parts–the tongue body and the tongue root which are divided by a groove shaped like the Chinese character for "person (人) " (Fig. 1-1).

The anterior portion of the tongue is called the tongue tip[1] while the posterior portion is known as the tongue root[2]. The middle [3] of the tongue is called the tongue middle and the sides of tongue

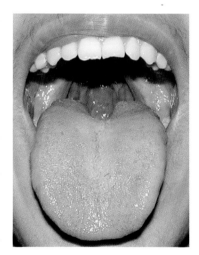

Fig. 1-1 ▲

are described as the tongue margins [4]. There is a vague striation in the center of the surface of the tongue which is defined as the midline groove[5] (Fig. 1-2).

When the tongue is rolled upward, the underside can be viewed. A fold of membrane that runs along the midline of the bottom of the tongue and is attached the bottom of oral cavity is called the frenulum. There are two long sublingual vessels found on either side of it (Fig. 1-3). The sublingual caruncle is located at the end of frenulum, and at its top is a pore common to the sublingual and submandibular

glands. Chinese medicine refers to the left side as the "golden fluid" (jīn jīn, 金津) and the right side as the "jade humor" (yù yè, 玉液). This is the passageway by which

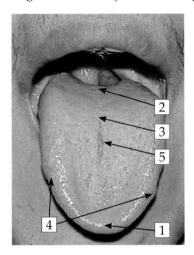

Fig. 1-2 ▲

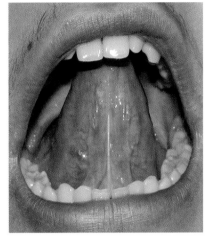

Fig. 1-3 ▲

stomach fluid and kidney essence move upward toward the tongue.

The tongue is covered with a semi-transparent mucus membrane which is very rough on the back of the tongue. A series of small cone shaped projections called tongue papillae are also located on the tongue back. There are four kinds of papillae: filiform papillae [1], fungiform papillae [2], circumvallate papillae [3] and foliate papillae [4]. The first two play an important role in forming the appearance of the tongue while the latter two are connected with taste (Fig. 1-4).

The number of filiform papillae is greater than the others, and they are distributed on the tongue tip, body and margins. Their shape is cylindrical and they are 0.5-2.5mm in height (Fig. 1-5). Their stratified squamous epithelium is often keratinized and sloughs off mixing with retained food and saliva to form a thin, white fur called a tongue coating (Fig. 1-6). The color and shape of the epithelium will change with the state of health.

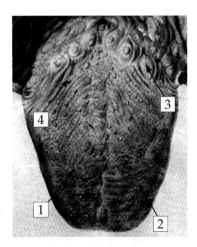

Fig. 1-4 ▲

Fungiform papillae are few in number. They are found near the tongue tip scattered among the filiform papillae and are shaped like a fungus. Their base is narrow with a circular top, and they are 0.5-1.5mm in height. The surface of their epithelium is smooth. Taste buds can sometimes be seen. The membrane is typically full of blood vessels. The papillae therefore assume a red color (Fig. 1-7); upon inspection by the naked eye, they present as small red dots (Fig. 1-8). Changes in the shape and color/luster of fungiform papillae are the main factors in changes in the quality of the tongue.

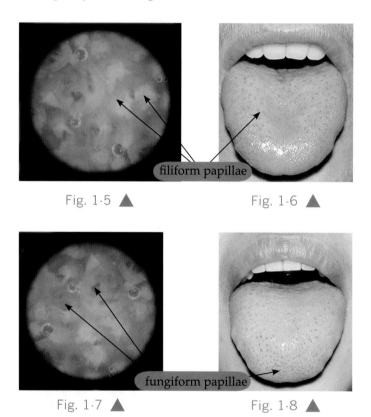

filiform papillae

Fig. 1·5 ▲   Fig. 1·6 ▲

fungiform papillae

Fig. 1·7 ▲   Fig. 1·8 ▲

2. Physiological Functions

The tongue has the ability to mix food, feel, taste and regulate the voice.

As a muscular organ, the tongue can move flexibly allowing food to be mixed completely in the oral cavity. In addition, there are many nerve endings in the circumvallate and foliate papillae that help the tongue to feel and taste fully.

Atlas of
Tongue
Diagnosis

Imperial Treasure Classic-Discussion of Methods for Determining Deficiency and Excess, Cold and Heat, Existence and Exhaustion, and Prognosis for Syndromes of the Small Intestine (Zhōng Zàng Jīng-Lùn Xiǎo Cháng Xū Shí Hán Rè Shēng Sǐ Nì Shùn Mài Zhèng Zhī Fǎ, 中藏经·论小肠虚实寒热生死逆顺脉证之法) says, "if the tongue is functioning harmoniously, speech is coherent and it is possible to distinguish flavors". Color Guide to Differentiating the Tongue-Lingual Papillae (Cǎi Tú Biàn Shé Zhǐ Nán-Shé Zhī Rǔ Tóu, 彩图辨舌指南·舌之乳头) points out specifically, *"near the tongue root lined up in the shape of the Chinese character for person (人), larger than the others, and full of nerve endings for taste are what are called taste buds".* The flexibility of the tongue and ability it has to move on its own and its ability to match articulations from the thoracic cavity and vocal cords make speech clear and smooth.

THE RELATIONSHIP BETWEEN THE TONGUE AND THE ZANG-FU ORGANS, THE CHANNELS AND COLLATERALS, AND THE QI, BLOOD AND BODY FLUIDS

Even though the tongue is an organ located in the oral cavity, it is closely related to the *zang-fu* organs, channels and collaterals, qi, blood and body fluids.

1. The Relationship between the Tongue and the *Zang-Fu* Organs and the Channels and Collaterals

The tongue body is linked to the many internal organs via the channels and collaterals. It is the sprout of the heart. The *Spiritual Pivot-Consideration of the Pulse (Líng Shū-Mài Dù, 灵枢·脉度)* says, "the heart qi corresponds with the tongue, and if it is functioning harmoniously, the tongue can taste five flavors." The *Spiritual Pivot-Channels (Líng Shū-Jīng Mài, 灵枢·经脉)* says, "the *shaoyin* channel of the hand passes through the heart and links to the tongue". Because the heart rules the blood

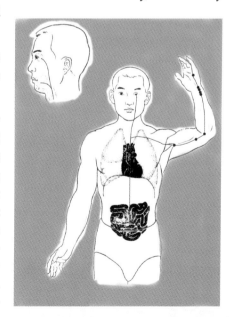

Fig. 1-9 ▲

and vessels that are abundant under the tongue, the heart blood rises upward to nourish the tongue. The circulation of the qi and blood is therefore reflected in the quality of the tongue. Because the heart rules the mind, and the mind commands the tongue, the tongue is closely connected to the mind. Therefore, the tongue, heart and mind can all be reflected in the appearance of the tongue (Fig. 1-9).

The tongue is regarded as the outward manifestation of the spleen. The *taiyin* channel of the foot links to the tongue which rules taste. Those points are supported by various quotations. For example, The *Spiritual Pivot-Consideration of the Pulse* (*Líng Shū-Mài Dù*, 灵枢·脉度) says, "*Spleen qi passes through the mouth. If the spleen is functioning harmoniously, then the mouth will recognize the five flavors.*" For this reason, it is said that the mouth is the orifice of the spleen. *The Spiritual Pivot-Channels* (*Líng Shū-Jīng Mài*, 灵枢·经脉) says, "*Taiyin channel of the foot...is connected to the root of the tongue, and disperses below the tongue*". In Chinese medicine, the spleen rules transportation and transformation, and the normal tongue depends heavily upon the nourishment of qi and blood; therefore the tongue reflects the exuberance and decline of qi and blood and is related to the spleen (Fig. 1-10).

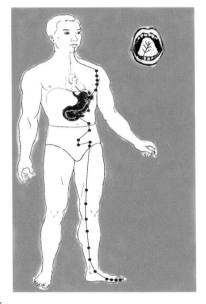

Fig. 1-10 ▲

The liver stores blood and rules the tendons while the kidney stores the essence. Thus, the *Spiritual Pivot-Channels* (*Líng Shū-Jīng Mài*, 灵枢·经脉) says, "*the liver corresponds to the tendons which assemble in the urethra and genitals, and its channel links to the tongue*".

Fig. 1-11 ▶

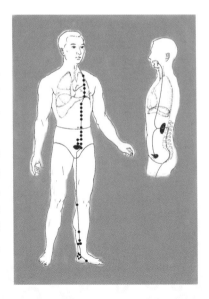

"The shaoyin channel of the foot travels upward and around the diaphragm, passes through the lung, crosses the throat and links to the tongue." (Fig. 1-11). The lung channel passes through pharynx and connects with the root of the tongue. The lung, intestines and gallbladder are linked indirectly to the tongue with the help of attached channels. In addition, the tongue is joined to the esophagus and connects to the stomach with the aid of the esophagus. Therefore, diseases of the *zang-fu* organs can be diagnosed by observation of the tongue.

2. The Relationship Between the Tongue and the Qi, Blood and Body Fluids

The heart rules the blood and is the supreme monarch of all organs. The spleen stores the nutritive blood and is the foundation of acquired constitution. The tongue is the sprout of the heart and is the manifestation of the spleen. The waxing and waning of the blood is therefore manifested in the tongue (Fig. 1-12, Fig. 1-13). The engorgement of the heart with qi and blood will result in a red, moist tongue, and deficient qi and blood of the spleen will lead to a pale tongue. The tongue coating, produced by the steaming of stomach qi, exhibits the functioning of the *zang-fu* organs (Fig. 1-14, Fig. 1-15). The first is an example of is stomach qi moving upward resulting in a thin white fur, and the second is an example of obstruction of the qi of the *fu* organs resulting in a hardening of the fur. In addition, under the tongue is the passageway by which the stomach *jin* (津) and kidney *ye* (液) flow

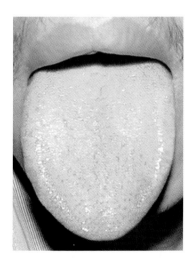

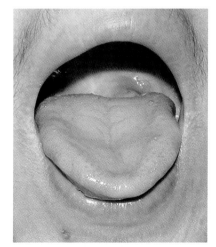

Fig. 1-12 ▲   Fig. 1-13 ▲

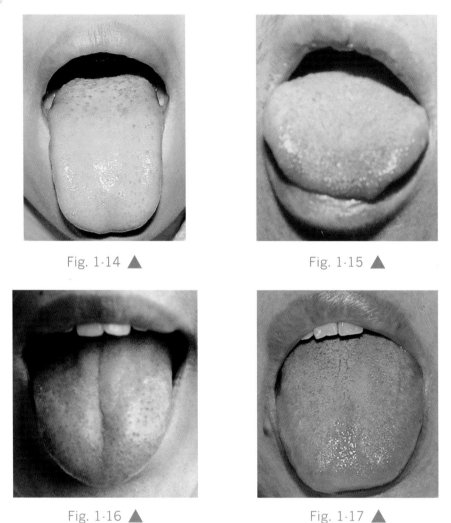

Fig. 1·14 ▲

Fig. 1·15 ▲

Fig. 1·16 ▲

Fig. 1·17 ▲

upwards. Just as the *Spiritual Pivot-Discussion of Distention* (*Líng Shū-Zhàng Lùn*, 灵枢·胀论) says, "*the spring of the jade fluid is the passageway of the jin ye*". For this reason, the amount of body fluids is reflected in the tongue (Fig. 1-16, Fig. 1-17). The first tongue is engorged with body fluids with a moist fur, and the second is deficent in body fluids with a dry fur.

Pathological changes in the *zang-fu* organs are reflected on the surface of the tongue. There are many ancient works that address the basic rules of tongue diagnosis, and they all reflect the following idea: the quality of the tongue is the

main way to look for disease in the five *zang*, and it focuses on the blood level; the tongue coat is the main way to look for disease in the six *fu*, and it focuses on the qi level. The tongue tip reflects pathology in the upper *jiao* which includes the heart and lung; the root of the tongue reflects pathology in the lower *jiao* which includes the kidney; the tongue margins reflect pathology in the liver and gallbladder.

In conclusion, the tongue is small and closely related to the *zang-fu* organs, the channels and collaterals, and the qi, blood, and body fluids. It can reflect physiological functioning and pathological changes objectively and flexibly. Just as it says in *Guide to Cold Damage-Methods of Pattern Differentiation by Inspecting the Tongue* (*Shāng Hán Zhǐ Zhǎng-Chá Shé Biàn Zhèng Fǎ*, 伤寒指掌·察舌辨症法), "*all diseases will be exhibited on the tongue, whether the disease exists in the channels and collaterals, the zang-fu organs, the ying-nutrient and wei-defense, or the qi and blood, whether the disease is exterior or interior, yin or yang, cold or hot, deficient or excess.*" *Clinically Efficacious Methods for Examining the Tongue* (*Lín Zhèng Yàn Shé Fǎ*, 临证验舌法) states, "*the tongue is the sprout of the heart, the commander of the five zang and the six fu. The heart qi crosses the tongue and opens into this orifice, a map to all the zang-fu organs that can be checked. Of the spleen, lung, liver and kidney, there is not one that does not connect to the heart. Assess the channels and collaterals, and examine the hand and foot yangming. There is no channel that does not pass through the tongue. Therefore, regarding ailments of the zang-fu organs and of the channels and collaterals, not only cold damage with fever and a visible tongue coat, but all miscellaneous signs of internal damage, there is not one that does not present in the shape or color of the tongue.*"

Section 2
Methods of Tongue Diagnosis and Items to Note

Tongue observation involves observing the appearance of the whole tongue systematically. Although the tongue can take on a variety of appearances, a doctor can analyze pathogenesis, summarize patterns and understand abnormal changes if he masters the basic methods of tongue diagnosis and understand the meaning of the properties of the tongue.

BASIC TONGUE DIAGNOSIS

Tongue diagnosis mainly refers to observation of the tongue. Sometimes inquiry and palpation (which includes touching, feeling, wiping and scraping) are also necessary for clinic diagnosis.

1. Basic Posture When Observing the Tongue

When observing the tongue, the patient should face natural light and sit up straight (patients with a serious disease can lie on their backs) with the head lifted slightly upward and the mouth open enough for natural light to reach the oral cavity so that the tongue can be inspected carefully. The doctor should also ask the patient to extend the tongue while relaxing and flattening it with the tongue tip curling down. These requirements are favorable to careful observation (Fig. 1-18). The doctor should sit directly opposite the patient (Fig. 1-19).

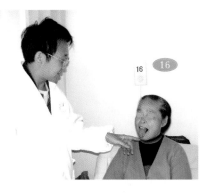

Fig. 1-18 ▲   Fig. 1-19 ▲

Regarding extending the tongue, special attention should be paid to the following points. The patient should make sure the tongue is relaxed to avoid overextension and curvature of the tongue that might result in a darkening of the color and a compaction of the coating (Fig. 1-20). At the same time, the tongue should not be extended for too long because blood circulation to the tongue can be affected turning it a bluish purple. *Guide to Diagnosing the*

Atlas of
Tongue
Diagnosis

Tongue-Differentiating the Tongue Coating (Biàn Shé Zhǐ Nán-Biàn Shé Zhǐ Tài Gòu, 辨舌指南・辨舌之苔垢) points out that the color of a normal tongue is light red. However, with too much exertion, it can become deep red. If the posture taken when extending the tongue varies, the tongue coating can exhibit different qualities such as tightness, sharpness, looseness, softness or even spikes caused by excess binding (Fig. 1-21). Patients must be trained several times to relax and flatten the tongue body completely.

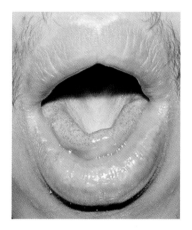

Fig. 1-20 ▲

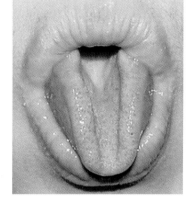

Fig. 1-21 ▲

2. Basic Procedures for Observing the Tongue

The order in which the tongue is to be observed is tip, middle, bilateral margins and finally the root. When observing the quality of the tongue, the tongue body is to be observed first followed by the tongue coating so as not to make a false assessment of the tongue body if the tongue is extended for too long. The tongue body and coat as well as individual features of the tongue should be assessed one by one.

When a doctor examines the quality of the tongue, emphasis should be placed on inspecting abnormal changes in the color, shape and movement of the tongue. When inspecting the tongue coating, one must begin with its absence or presence, its color and luster and the quality of the coating as well as the distribution of these conditions. Finally, when necessary, the sublingual veins should be inspected.

3. Helpful Techniques for Observing the Tongue

(1) Touching and Feeling

If the doctor is uncertain when observing the tongue, it is necessary to combine it with other diagnostic methods. For example, the tongue can be touched or felt to verify the moistness or dryness of the coating. After making sure the hands are clean, the doctor can touch the tongue with the index finger (Fig. 1-22). Touching refers to pressing a certain area on the surface of tongue two to three times to see the degree of damp polluting the belly of the tongue.

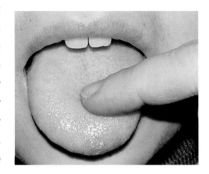

Fig. 1-22 ▲

Feeling refers to sliding your index finger from the root to the tip of tongue one to three times. This not only for the purpose of inspecting for damp polluting the belly of the tongue, but is sometimes necessary to feel for the presence of prickles on the tongue belly. It is a way of distinguishing the degree of roughness or stickiness in the tongue quality and coating (Fig. 1-23).

Fig. 1-23 ▲

(2) Wiping and Scraping

In clinical practice, wiping and scraping are mainly used to ascertain how tightly the coating is affixed to the tongue (whether the coating rooted or not) as well as the putridity and greasiness of the tongue coating. What looks like dryness can in fact be moistness when scraped. This kind of coating is called a false coating. It is a sign of dampness obstructing the qi and a failure to distribute body fluids. If the coating is thick and easily removed by wiping, its quality is loose and putrid. Moreover, if it is scraped and does not come off, this quality is known as tight and greasy. After wiping and scraping, if there is no coating on the tongue, this is called un-rooted. If there is only a little coating, it is still regarded as a rooted coating. *Guide to Tongue Differentiation-Differentiating the*

Atlas of
Tongue
Diagnosis

Tongue Coating (*Biàn Shé Zhǐ Nán-Biàn Shé Zhǐ Tāi Gòu*, 辨舌指南・辨舌之苔垢) points out, "*the method for distinguishing moistness, dryness, roughness and greasiness should be wiping and scraping*".

When scraping, a doctor should use a sanitized scraper or tongue depressor to slowly scrape the coating with moderate strength from the root to the tip of tongue. This should be done three to five times (Fig. 1-24).

Fig. 1-24 ▲

In order to wipe the tongue correctly, a piece of disinfected cloth is needed. The cloth should be wound around the index finger, soaked in clear or peppermint water and used to wipe the tongue from the root to the tip. This should be repeated four to five times in a row (Fig. 1-25).

Fig. 1-25 ▲

During the procedure, an appropriate amount of strength should be used. Too little pressure will result in leaving coating that would otherwise come off while too much pressure will result in the removal of all the coating. In addition, the tongue is easily injured. After scraping and wiping, the loss and regeneration of the coating should be inspected carefully. Secondly, although the diagnostic significance of each technique is similar, the pressure used for scraping is great compared to the pressure used for wiping. For this reason, scraping is appropriate for relatively tight, concentrated, thick and greasy coatings, and wiping is appropriate for relatively superficial, transparent, loose and putrid coatings. In general, it is good to first used wiping, and if there is no result, to then use scraping.

In addition, if the color of the coating has been affected by food or medications, the doctor should combine an examination of the tongue with information obtained during the interview about diet, medications and the taste in the mouth etc. When observing the movement of the tongue, the doctor can ask the patient

to turn the tongue or speak etc. in order to determine whether the tongue body is flexible or to look for other conditions such as crookedness. The doctor can also inquire whether the patient feels pain, numbness or any other sensations.

OTHER ITEMS TO PAY ATTENTION TO IN TONGUE DIAGNOSIS

Tongue diagnosis forms an important basis for clinical diagnosis in Chinese medicine. In order to insure that it is performed correctly and that the information gathered is accurate, careful attention must be paid to the following points when inspecting the tongue.

1. Lighting Conditions

When inspecting the tongue, it is of primary importance to pay attention to the lighting. Lighting seriously affects the color of the tongue. The same tongue can appear to be different colors under different lighting, and slight carelessness can lead to a wrong impression resulting in a misdiagnosis. Just as it says in *Guide to Tongue Differentiation-Methods of Observing the Tongue* (*Biàn Shé Zhǐ Nán-Guān Shé Zhī Xīn Fǎ*, 辨舌指南 · 观舌之心法), "*under lamp light, a yellow coating can appear white. Even though the tongue can serve as evidence, it can also fail to settle matters. Without careful inspection, it is difficult to avoid making mistakes in treatment*".

It is best to observe the tongue in the daytime under full and soft natural light because those conditions are most conducive to tongue diagnosis (Fig. 1-26). In addition, observation of the tongue should be performed away from direct sunlight, and the poor light on cloudy days or colored lamplight should be avoided.

Fig. 1-26 ▲

2. The Influence of Diet and Medications

Food and medications can also directly influence the appearance of the tongue.

Many kinds of food and drink can change the appearance of the tongue coating.

Atlas of
Tongue
Diagnosis

For example, milk and soy milk can cause the coating to become thick and white (Fig. 1-27). Oranges, vitamin B2 and herbal decoctions can turn the coating yellow (Fig. 1-28). Sour plum juice, coffee, nutritional supplements containing iron, and long-term smoking will all turn the coating black (Fig. 1-29).

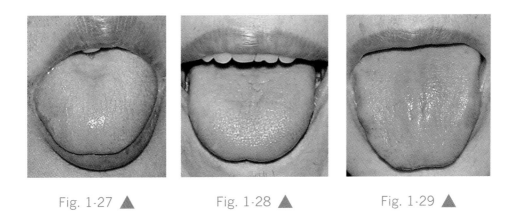

Fig. 1-27 ▲   Fig. 1-28 ▲   Fig. 1-29 ▲

Some stimulating foods like hot peppers, ginger and other pungent foods along with fried foods bring blood to the tongue and cause it to turn a deep red (Fig. 1-30). Long term consumption of some antibiotics can lead to a black, greasy coating or to a moldy, curd-like coating (Fig. 1-31).

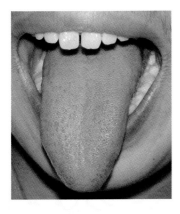

Fig. 1-30 ▲

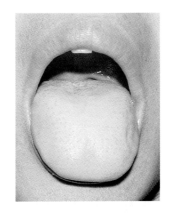

Fig. 1-31 ▲

3. Effect of the Oral Cavity on the Appearance of the Tongue

Tooth loss can cause the coating to become thicker on side of the tooth loss (Fig. 1-32). Dental inlays can cause teeth marks on the sides of the tongue (Fig. 1-33).

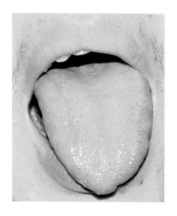

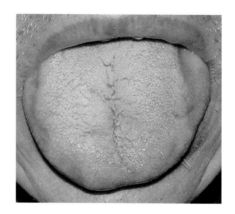

Fig. 1-32 ▲   Fig. 1-33 ▲

Section 3
Basic Information on Tongue Diagnosis and the Appearance of the Normal Tongue

BASIC INFORMATION ON TONGUE DIAGNOSIS

Tongue diagnosis includes observation of both the tongue body and the coating. The quality refers to the body of tongue that is made of muscles and vessels (Fig. 1-34). Observing the quality of the tongue requires observation of abnormal changes in the vitality, color, shape and movement of the tongue body in order to discern deficiency or excess of the *zang-fu* organs and the prosperity or decline of the qi and blood.

The tongue coating consists of the thin fur-like material found on the tongue body in normal, healthy people (Fig. 1-34). Observation of the tongue coating includes looking at changes in its color and quality in order to determine the nature of disease, the depth of the disease, and the waxing and waning of evil versus normal qi. The *Guide to Tongue Differentiation* states, *"The excess and deficiency of zang-fu organs can be determined on the basis of tongue quality while looking at the tongue coating allows one to determine the depth of the evil"*. It also says that *"excess and deficiency of yin and yang can be verified by observing the quality of the tongue while the coldness, hotness and the depth of the evil can be determined by looking at the coating"*. Synthesizing changes in the tongue quality and coat is what is known as the appearance of the tongue. It is through summarizing and analyzing the changes that we can understand disease completely and supply the correct information needed for clinical practice.

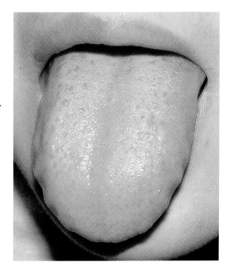

Fig. 1-34 ▲

Tongue vitality includes thriving or withering; tongue color includes light red, pale, red, crimson, purple and blue; tongue shape includes enlargement and thinness, toughness and tenderness, cracks and prickles; the tongue condition includes flaccidity and stiffness, protrusion and retraction, crookedness and trembling etc.

The tongue coating is called "tongue embryo" in *Discussion of Cold Damage*. There is a paragraph in *Exploration of Exterior Diagnosis of Appearance-Pattern Differentiation in Cold Damage Tongue Coatings* (*Xíng Sè Wài Zhěn Jiǎn Mó-Shāng Hán Shé Tāi Biàn Zhèng*, 形色外诊简摩·伤寒舌苔辨证) cited from *Introduction to Cold Damage* (*Shāng Hán Xù Lùn*, 伤寒绪论) that says, *"the term tongue embryo first originated from Zhang Zhong-jing (张仲景). It is here that the evil qi congeals. It is as if it was conceived here, and for this reason, it is called an embryo"*. Tongue coating colors include white, yellow, gray and black. Qualities of the tongue coating include thickness and thinness, moistness and dryness, looseness and tightness, evenness of distribution, concentration and dispersion, peeled, rootedness and un-rootedness of the coating.

In addition, under special conditions, it is necessary to examine the sublingual veins by looking at their length, thickness, shape and color.

APPEARANCE OF THE NORMAL TONGUE

In order to distinguish abnormal changes in the appearance of the tongue, it is first necessary to grasp the normal appearance of the tongue. Only if the normal is understood is it possible to identify changes.

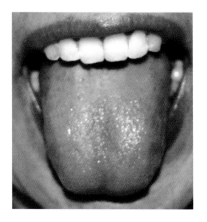

The normal tongue is characterized as a middle sized, soft, neither tough nor tender, free moving, light red, and covered by a thin and even white coating of moderate moistness which cannot be scraped away and is rooted to the tongue. It is usually summarized as "light red tongue with a thin white coating" (Fig. 1-35).

Fig. 1-35 ▲

As to the principles of how the appearance of the normal tongue arises, *Systematic Records on Tongue Coating* (*Shé Tāi Tŏng Zhì*, 舌胎统志) says, "*The tongue is the sprout of the heart. The color is red and not delicate; the quality is moist but not glossy; the appearance is of coating without prickles; and the overall appearance must be light red with a thin white coating. This is a tongue that not harboring evil*". In addition, "*the color of the tongue is light red and this is normal for most people…red is of the qi of the heart and pale is of the stomach qi*". The *General Introduction to Tongue Inspection* (*Shé Jiàn Zŏng Lùn*, 舌鉴总论) says, "*The tongue is the sprout of the heart, and the heart belongs to fire. Its color is red and it resides in the lung, The lung belongs to metal and its color is white. For this reason, the quality of the tongue is light red and the coating slightly white. Moreover, the red must be red and moist, and the white must be a slight coating that is not thick, or slightly thick and peeled. Naturally, dryness and dampness should be moderate and the coating should not be slippery or dry. This is a healthy tongue, or the appearance of fire stored within metal*". *Original Meaning of the Discussion of Cold Damage-Differentiating Tongue Coating* (*Shāng Hán Lùn Běn Zhǐ-Biàn Shé Tāi*, 伤寒论本旨 · 辨舌苔) says, "*The tongue coating is a manifestation of the generation of qi in the stomach, and stomach qi is a product of*

the heart and spleen. For this reason, a healthy person typically has a thin coating that is qi that has arisen from the stomach like little shoots of grass". This explains how the normal appearance of the tongue takes shape, and is intimately related to the normal activities of *zang-fu* organs functioning. The normal tongue appearance is a manifestation of exuberant stomach qi, harmonious qi and blood and the normal functioning of the *zang-fu* organs.

PHYSIOLOGICAL CHANGES IN THE TONGUE

With changes in the internal and external environment, the tongue will change accordingly. Thus, it is necessary to understand some of the physiological changes that can occur in the tongue in order to make accurate clinical diagnoses.

1. The Factors of Age and Sex

Age is one of the factors producing physiological changes in the appearance of the tongue. Due to differences in age, the appearance of the tongue will necessarily exhibit variations. For example, young children have "tender yin" or "tender yang" constitutions, and the spleen and stomach functions have not fully developed. In addition, they are growing quickly and the necessary nutrients acquired from food are in relatively short supply. For this reason, the tongue quality is often pale and tender (Fig. 1-36), and there tends to be little tongue coating that peels easily. The *zang-fu* organs, essence and qi of elderly people are in decline, and the qi and blood tend to be deficient while transportation is relatively slow. For this reason, the color of the tongue tends to be dark red (Fig. 1-37).

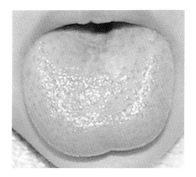

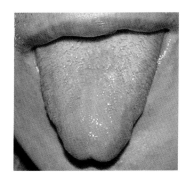

Fig. 1-36 ▲   Fig. 1-37 ▲

The sex of a person has no bearing on the tongue in most cases, but in females, because of the physiological influences of the menstrual cycle, fungiform papillae full of blood can appear during the period and the tongue quality can tend to be red with enlarged prickles on the tip. After the period, these phenomena all disappear by themselves (Fig. 1-38).

Fig. 1-38 ▶

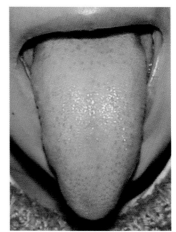

2. Constitutional and Congenital Factors

Because of different preexisting congenital factors and differences in constitution, there are variations in the appearance of the tongue. Just like *Guide to Differentiating the Tongue* points out, *"For tongues without disease, each has its own form. There are clean ones, ones with only a little coating, ones that are fresh red, ones that are pale, or ones that are tense and pointed, or ones that are loose and soft as well as ones with teeth marks. Because there is no disease present, each of these tongues exhibits congenital differences and it is for this reason that the quality of the tongues differ."* It is as in the case of overweight people where the tongue is enlarged and pale (Fig. 1-39), or the case of thin people where the tongue tends to be thin and red (Fig. 1-40).

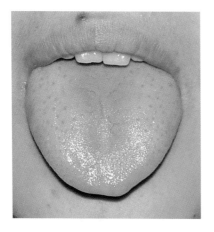

Fig. 1-39 ▲

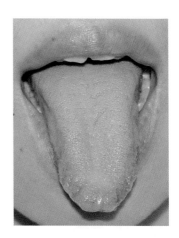

Fig. 1-40 ▲

In addition, the congenitally cracked tongue (Fig. 1-41) the tongue with teeth marks (Fig. 1-42) and the geographic tongue (Fig. 1-43) are primarily seen when a person is congenitally deficient or has a weak constitution. Although they might not have obvious clinical symptoms for a long time, these congenital traits can be a potential factor in the susceptibility to and type of disease in any type of pathogenesis, and can influence the ability to get through an illness or the prognosis for an illness.

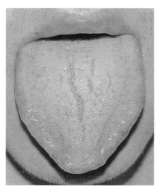
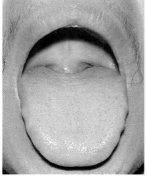
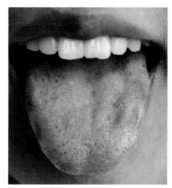

Fig. 1-41 ▲   Fig. 1-42 ▲   Fig. 1-43 ▲

3. Climatic and Environmental Factors

Differences in season and region produce changes in climate and environment, and these factors necessarily lead to changes in the appearance of the tongue. *As Guide to Differentiating the Tongue-Principles of Differentiating How Tongue Quality Gives Rise to Coat* (*Biàn Shé Zhǐ Nán-Biàn Shé Zhì Shēng Tāi Zhī Yuán Lǐ*, 辨舌指南·辨舌质生苔之原理) points out, "*There is a layer of superficial white coat on the tongues of most people, or a layer of superficial yellow coating. Damp earth is active in the summer so the coating will be relatively thick and slightly yellow, but not too filled up and clogged.*" In the summer, damp is flourishing and the tongue coating easily becomes thick, the color of the coating is often pale yellow (Fig. 1-44). Likewise, pathogenic dryness is active in the fall and the coat will tend to be thin and dry (Fig. 1-45). It is cold in the winter, and the coating is often relatively damp and moist (Fig. 1-46).

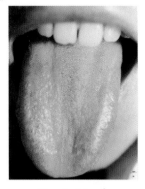

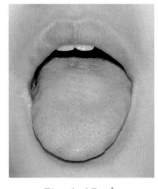

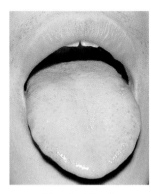

Fig. 1-44 ▲   Fig. 1-45 ▲   Fig. 1-46 ▲

In the Southeast of China, the climate is relatively damp and hot. The Northwestern and Northeastern areas are cold and dry. These geographic differences influence the production of different appearances of the tongue. The appearance of the tongue is a reflection of the relationship between the body's physiological activities and the natural world.

4. Factors of Daily Lifestyle and Habits

Changes in diet and daily life can influence the appearance of the tongue. For example, the tongue coating is thicker in the morning (Fig. 1-47) and thinner after eating (Fig. 1-48). After taking part in activities that require physical strength, the tongue is at its reddest and most vivid (Fig. 1-49). *Guide to Differentiating the Tongue-Preface* (*Biàn Shé Zhǐ Nán-Xù Yán*, 辨舌指南·绪言) states, "*People eat three meals a day and for this reason, the coating changes three times per day. This is what is called a lively tongue with no appearance of disease.*"

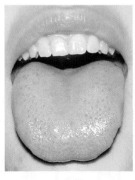

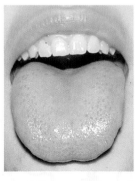

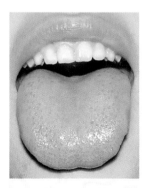

Fig. 1-47 ▲   Fig. 1-48 ▲   Fig. 1-49 ▲

Atlas of
Tongue
Diagnosis

Habits of daily lifestyle and addictions to food and drink will interfere with the appearance of the tongue. For example, a person who likes to smoke usually has a brown coating (Fig. 1-50); a person who likes to drink alcohol often has a yellow, greasy coating (Fig. 1-51); a person who favors tea often has a damp, moist tongue (Fig. 1-52); a person who opens his mouth to breath often has a dry coating (Fig. 1-53); people accustomed to scraping their tongue will have a thick coating that becomes thin (Fig. 1-54); for people who have been prohibited from eating food for a long time, the coating will accumulate and become thick (Fig. 1-55).

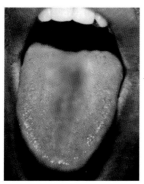

Fig. 1-50 ▲

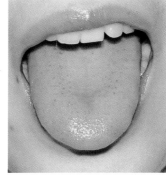

Fig. 1-51 ▲

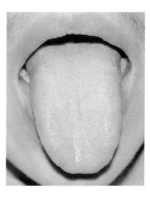

Fig. 1-52 ▲

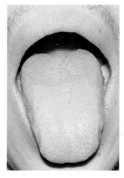

Fig. 1-53 ▲

Fig. 1-54 ▲

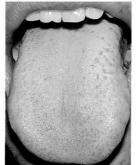

Fig. 1-55 ▲

Aside from this, it is valuable to note that among that normal people who have an abnormal tongue, with the exception of the above mentioned physiological factors, there is a portion that may be experiencing the initial symptoms of a potential disease. Since the tongue can reflect pathological changes in the interior quickly and sensitively, the tongue of a person with an interior pathology will undergo acute changes before recognizable symptoms become apparent. Because of this, when we find a normal person with an abnormal tongue in clinical practice, it is of primary importance to combine diagnosis through inquiry, cautious differentiation, and sincere analysis to see if they are real physiological changes or evidence of a hidden pathological condition on the tongue before the appearance of symptoms. It is necessary to carry out regular follow up visits with the patient.

CHAPTER TWO

Diagnosing Tongue Quality

The tongue quality, also called the tongue body, consists of muscles, arteries and veins, and tissue. In diagnosing the quality of the tongue, it is of primary importance to examine its vitality, color, shape and appearance as well as the sublingual veins.

Section 1
Diagnosing Tongue Vitality

The vitality of the tongue, since it is the expression of the tongue, is a manifestation of the body's life activities on the tongue. After examining what the tongue spirit does and does not display, an overall assessment can be made of the prosperity and decline of the vitality of the *zang-fu* organs, of the success or failure of the organism's chance of survival, of the ferocity of the illness, and of other basic situations. *Diagnosing According to the Channels-Outline of Diagnostic Methods of Observing the Tongue (Wàng Zhěn Zūn Jīng-Wàng Shé Zhěn Fǎ Tí Gāng,* 望诊遵经 · 望舌诊法提纲*) points out, "A person with a tongue that possesses vitality will live while a person with a tongue that lacks vitality will die. No matter the changes [in the tongue], it must have vitality and cannot be without it for even an instant".*

The basic characteristics of tongue vitality manifest in the color and movement of the tongue body.

POSSESSING VITALITY

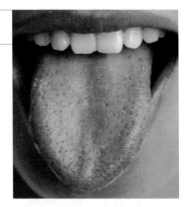

Features: Red tongue body that is lively, bright and moist with flexible movement (Fig. 2-1).

Mechanism: Tongue body has spirit that shows that the yin, yang, qi and blood all have sufficient essence and that is full of vitality.

Significance: A sign of health; even though there are symptoms of illness, the prognosis is good.

Fig. 2-1 ▲

LACKING VITALITY

Features: The tongue lacking vitality refers to a dark, withered tongue body that is rigid and stiff (Fig. 2-2).

Mechanism: The tongue body lacks spirit which shows a loss of yin, yang, qi and blood and that there is little vitality.

Significance: The disease is serious and the prognosis is bad.

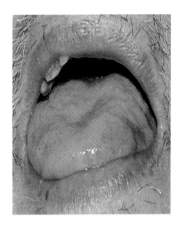

Guides to Differentiating the Tongue - Differentiating Tongue Vitality (Biàn Shé Zhǐ Nán-Biàn Shé Zhī Shén Qì, 辨 舌指南·辨舌之神气) says, "The thriving tongue has luster and the prognosis is good. The withered tongue lacks vitality

Fig. 2-2 ▲

and the prognosis is bad. The thriving, moist tongue has sufficient fluids; the dry withered tongue lacks fluids. The thriving tongue has vitality...persons with a bright, moist tongue that is the color of blood will live. Persons with a dark, withered tongue that does not have the color of blood will die. All tongues with luster, no matter whether they have a yellow, gray or black coating, if on the inside they are red and moist when scraped, they are vital and thriving, and the prognosis is good for all diseases; if the tongue lacks luster and body, regardless of whether or not there is a coat, if when you look at the inside and see that it is withered and dark, and completely lacks vitality then the prognosis for any disease is bad." It is apparent from this that the vitality or lack thereof in the tongue is a reflection of the prosperity or decline of the *zang-fu* organs, the qi and blood, and the fluids, and is connected with the prognosis of the patient.

Section 2
Diagnosis of Tongue Color

Medically, the color of the tongue can be light red, pale, red, crimson, purple or blue. Apart from light red, the others are all categorized as pathological.

THE LIGHT RED TONGUE

Features: The tongue is light red and moist. It is neither light nor dark. (Fig. 2-3)

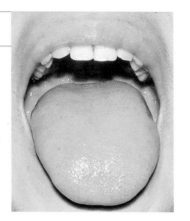

Fig. 2-3 ▶

Mechanism: The light red tongue is the natural color of the tongue body. *Systematic Records on Tongue Coating-The Light Red Tongue* (*Shé Tāi Tŏng Zhì-Dàn Hóng Shé*, 舌苔统志·淡红舌) says *"The average person has a light red tongue. Red reflects the heart qi and pale reflects the stomach qi"*. *Syndrome Differentiation in Tongue Examination-General Introduction to the Red Tongue* (*Shé Jiàn Biàn Zhèng-Hóng Shé Zŏng Lùn*, 舌鉴辨证·红舌总论) also says, *"the average person has a tongue that is a light red which is neither light nor dark."*

Significance: The light red tongue is often seen in healthy people, suggesting sufficiency of heart blood, exuberance of stomach qi, and harmony of the blood and qi. In the early stages of externally contracted disease, the light red tongue also shows that the disease has invaded the exterior muscle layer, but has not yet penetrated to the qi, blood or *zang-fu* organs and is classified as a mild case of disease.

THE PALE TONGUE

Features: Compared with the color of the normal tongue, the pale tongue looks lighter, is less red and more white (Fig. 2-4).

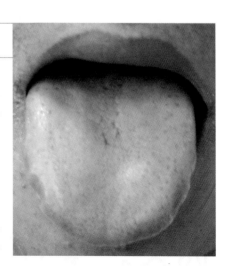

Fig. 2-4 ▶

Mechanism: Deficient qi and blood fail to nourish the tongue, or the decline of yang fails to send blood up to nourish the tongue, so the color becomes pale.

Significance: A pale tongue is usually seen in patients with deficiency of qi and blood or decline of yang.

The pale tongue takes on different characteristics and significance according to the amount and changes of the coating.

The pale tongue with a thin body is called a pale and thin tongue, and it results from the deficiency of both qi and blood, and the failure of the deficient blood to send nourishment up to the tongue (Fig. 2-5).

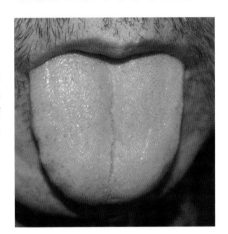

Fig. 2-5 ▶

A pale tongue that is withered with little fluid and is not the color of blood is called the withered white tongue (Fig. 2-6). It is due to an insufficiency of the qi and blood that usually results from a deficiency of yang that cannot transport blood, or the depletion of qi due to desertion of the blood.

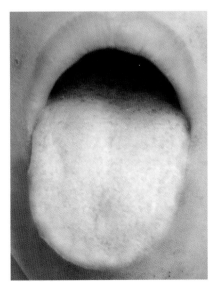

Fig. 2-6 ▶

A pale tongue with an extremely enlarged body, teeth marks on both sides, and a moist, wet surface with a lot of fluid is called a pale, enlarged, teeth marked tongue (Fig. 2-7). It usually results from internal retention of dampness due to yang deficiency.

A pale, glossy tongue without coating is called a pale glossy tongue (Fig. 2-8). It suggests the decline of spleen and stomach qi, and is a symptom of the waning of qi and blood.

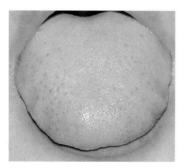

Fig. 2-7 ▲

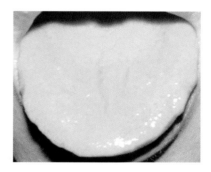

Fig. 2-8 ▲

THE RED TONGUE

Features: When the color of tongue is deeper than light red, it assumes a fresh red color (Fig. 2-9). This is known as a red tongue.

Mechanism: Heat in body makes qi and blood boil. The vessels of tongue then fill up. A red tongue is also the result of the upward invasion of deficient heat that results from depleted yin and fluids. For this reason, the tongue assumes a fresh red color.

Significance: This is primarily a heat syndrome.

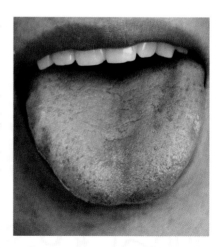

Fig. 2-9 ▲

Different sized tongue bodies and different tongue coatings suggest different pathologies.

⬤ A tongue with red margins and a red tip are caused by an externally contracted wind heat syndrome in the early stages (Fig. 2-10). The tip of the tongue reflects the heart and lung which belong to the upper *jiao*. Warm evil invades the lung and defensive qi first.

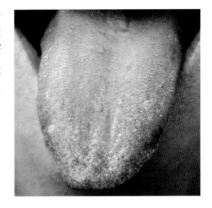

Fig. 2-10 ▶

⬤ A red tongue with rough and prickly coating on tip, or with a thick yellow coating primarily suggests an excess heat syndrome; it suggests extreme heat during a period of externally contracted disease (Fig. 2-11), and excess heat and yang of the *zang-fu* organs during a period of internal injury (Fig. 2-12). Due to enlarged blood vessels which are caused by flourishing heat and surging blood.

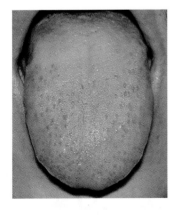

Fig. 2-11 ▲

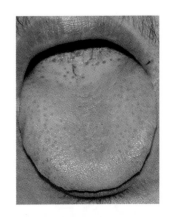

Fig. 2-12 ▲

◯ A withered red tongue with little or no coating, or with cracks in the body are resulted primarily from an upward invasion of deficient heat resulting from deficient yin (Fig. 2-13). Usually appears in chronic consumptive disease and the later stages of warm disease.

◯ A red tongue with a yellow greasy coating usually suggests heat with damp (Fig. 2-14). The heat causes the red color and damp causes the yellow greasy coating.

◯ A red tongue with a white coating like a pile of flour is due to a combination of externally contracted turbid damp evil combined with heat toxin (Fig. 2-15). The pathogenesis is damp heat accumulating.

◯ A red dry and thin tongue usually is due to hurt of fluid by excessive heat (Fig. 2-16).

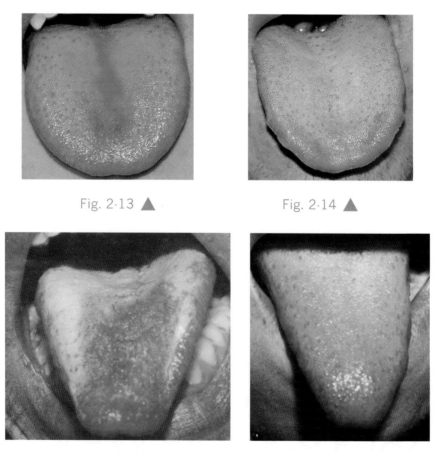

Fig. 2-13 ▲   Fig. 2-14 ▲

Fig. 2-15 ▲   Fig. 2-16 ▲

If only the tip of the tongue is red, it is due to heart fire flaring up (Fig. 2-17); a tongue with bilaterally red margins is due to liver and gallbladder heat (Fig. 2-18); a red tongue with a peeled coating suggests injury of the stomach yin (Fig. 2-19); a red tongue with a peeled coating at the root of the tongue (Fig. 2-20) is usually due to kidney yin deficiency. Since the condition of the *zang-fu* organs can be reflected in the appearance of the tongue, observation of the tongue allows one to make speculations about pathological changes in the internal organs.

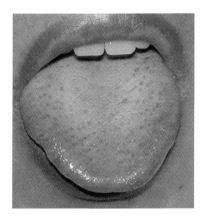

Fig. 2-17 ▲

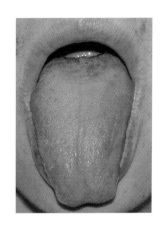

Fig. 2-18 ▲

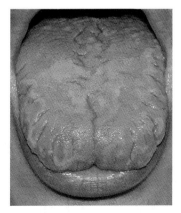

Fig. 2-19 ▲

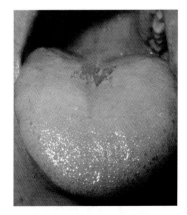

Fig. 2-20 ▲

Syndrome Differentiation by Inspecting the Tongue - Introduction to the Red Tongue (*Shé Jiàn Biàn Zhèng-Hóng Shé Zǒng Lùn*, 舌鉴辨证·红舌总论) points out, "*A red tongue can be seen in syndromes of the exterior and interior, of cold and heat, and of deficiency and excess. A bright red tongue suggests excess heat in the zang-fu organs. A purple red tongue means extreme heat in the zang-fu organs due to a seasonal illness or the misuse of warm tonics. A bright red tongue without any coating results from upward invasion of deficient heat due to deficiency of yin. A dry red tongue without any coating suggests exhaustion of the fluids and a deficiency of yin.*"

THE CRIMSON TONGUE

Features: The crimson tongue is a deep red tongue. The color is darker and more intense than that of the red tongue. It is often seen in cases of extreme fever (Fig. 2-21).

Mechanism: It results from an invasion of heat into *ying*-nutrient level and exhaustion of *ying*-nutrient yin, or the upward invasion of deficient heat due to deficiency of yin and exhaustion of fluids, or the exhaustion of yin where yin is damaged by heat and the blood becomes concentrated.

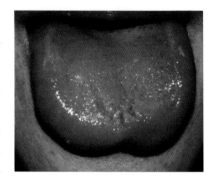

Fig. 2-21 ▲

Significance: Mainly heat flourishing. The crimson tongue appears both in diseases caused by external factors and diseases caused by internal factors; each of them has different features and significance.

    A dry crimson tongue, with or without prickles, which can be seen in externally contracted disease suggests an invasion of the *ying*-nutrient and *xue*-blood level by heat evil (Fig. 2-22, Fig. 2-23). *Guide to Differentiating the Tongue-Differenting Tongue Color* (*Biàn Shé Zhǐ Nán-Biàn Shé Zhī Yán Sè*, 辨舌指南·辨舌之颜色) says, "*When heat enters the ying-nutrient level, the tongue color will be crimson, and the crimson tongue suggests that warm heat evil has entered the ´ying-nutrient and xue-blood levels*".

    A crimson tongue with little or no coating, or with a crack is usually seen in internal injury, and suggests deficient heat resulting from depletion of yin and fluids (Fig. 2-24, Fig. 2-25); A crimson tongue with a transparent coating results from the exhaustion of stomach and kidney yin (Fig. 2-26, Fig. 2-27).

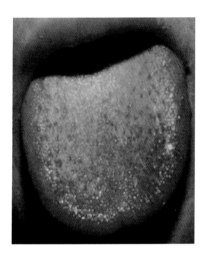

Fig. 2-22 ▲

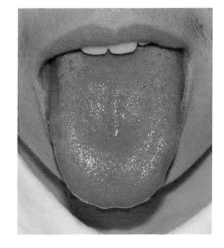

Fig. 2-23 ▲

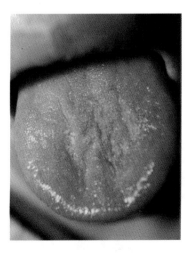

Fig. 2-24 ▲

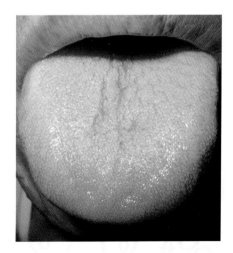

Fig. 2-25 ▲

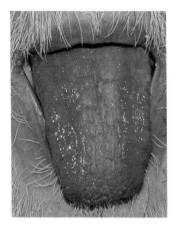

Fig. 2-26 ▲

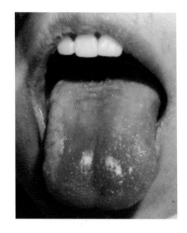

Fig. 2-27 ▲

THE PURPLE TONGUE

Features: Pale purple, crimson purple or bluish purple tongues are all called purple tongues (Fig. 2-28).

Mechanism: Purple tongues are usually caused by failure of the blood to move smoothly and the resulting stagnation from cold, heat, yang deficiency or the toxins in alcohol.

Significance: Indicates pathological changes of unsmooth circulation for qi and blood.

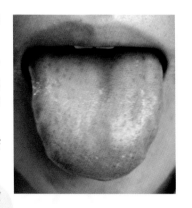

Fig. 2-28 ▲

A pale or dark, greasy, purple tongue suggests a cold syndrome while a withered, crimson, purple tongue with little fluid suggests a heat syndrome.

⬤ The pale purple tongue (Fig. 2-29) or dark and moist purple tongue (Fig. 2-30), results primarily from the stagnation of qi and blood caused by yang deficiency and cold flourishing in which the yang fails to warm and move them.

⬤ The withered, crimson, purple tongue is always due to injury of nutritive yin

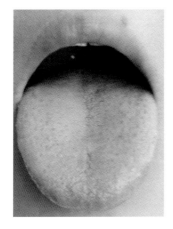

Fig. 2-29 ▲

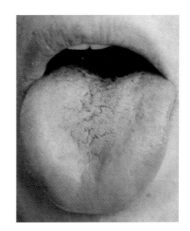

Fig. 2-30 ▲

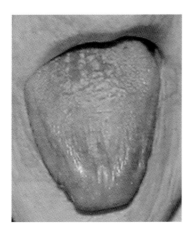

Fig. 2-31 ▲

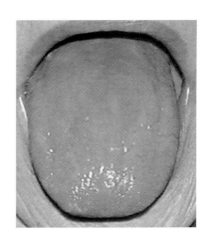

Fig. 2-32 ▲

caused by excess heat (Fig. 2-31).

   ◯ The purple and swollen tongue is due to the toxins in alcohol invading the heart (Fig. 2-32).

   ◯ When the tongue body is light blue and purple, it is called a bluish purple tongue, and it is mainly due to coagulated blood and stagnant qi that are a result of cold (Fig. 2-33).

A bluish purple tongue is also seen in congenital heart diseases (Fig. 2-34), and the syndromes that are caused by toxins from foods and drugs (Fig. 2-35).

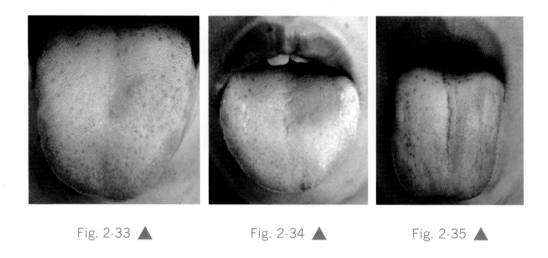

Fig. 2-33 ▲   Fig. 2-34 ▲   Fig. 2-35 ▲

THE BLUE TONGUE

Features: When the tongue is blue without any red color, it is called a blue tongue. In ancient times, it was called a "buffalo tongue".

Mechanism: A blue tongue often indicates the stagnation of yang by cold, or the deficiency of yang with a combination of cold or blood stasis.

Significance: Inhibited movement of blood.

The entirely blue tongue is due to a direct attack of cold on the liver or kidney, a decline in yang qi, or depression of the yang where it does not diffuse (Fig. 2-36).

Blue in the tongue margins is due to internal blood stasis (Fig. 2-37).

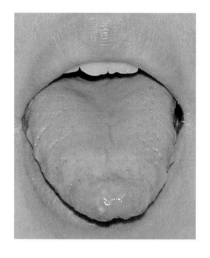

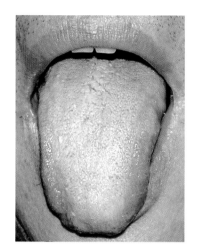

Fig. 2-36 ▲   Fig. 2-37 ▲

General Record of Tongue Coating considered the completely blue tongue with a dry mouth and desire to gargle but not swallow water to be a sign of blood stasis. *Guide to Differentiating the Tongue* considered the liver to belong to wood, and the blue color to be indicative of liver disease. Therefore, the blue tongue is a sign of a dangerous syndrome involving a toxin in the *jueyin* level.

Section 3
Diagnosis of the Tongue Shape

Tongue shape includes the quality and shape of the tongue. The normal shape of the tongue is soft and flexible, neither too big nor too small, and it should have luster and be moist. Abnormal changes in its shape include tenderness, toughness, prickles, teeth marks, cracks and so on.

THE TOUGH TONGUE

Features: The fissures on the tongue are rough and shrunken. The tongue is hard, and the color is relatively dark (Fig. 2-38).

Mechanism: It results from excess evil flooding the body, and when the normal qi is not yet exhausted, it fights with the evil. The evil qi causes stagnation in the upper *jiao*.

Significance: The tough tongue, no matter what color of its body, primarily indicates an excess syndrome. *Guide to Differentiating the Tongue* says *"A rough and sturdy tongue, no matter whether it has a yellow, gray or black coating, usually indicates an excess syndrome."*

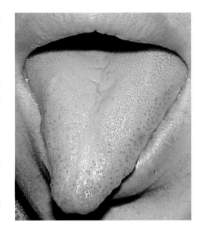

Fig. 2-38 ▲

THE TENDER TONGUE

Features: Fissures in the tongue body are subtle, superficial and plump, and the color of the tongue is pale (Fig. 2-39, Fig. 2-40).

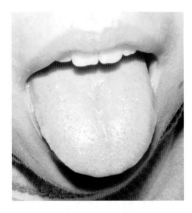

Fig. 2-39 ▲

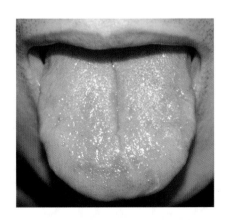

Fig. 2-40 ▲

Mechanism: It results from deficient qi and blood failing to fill the channels and collaterals in the tongue, or deficient yang failing to transport blood to nourish the tongue body, or deficient yang resulting in retention of cold damp.

Significance: The tender tongue, no matter the color of the body, is usually indicative of deficiency syndromes. *Guide to Differentiating the Tongue* says, "A tender tongue, no matter whether it has a gray, black, yellow or white coating, primarily indicates a deficiency syndrome".

THE ENLARGED TONGUE

Features: A relatively normal tongue body which is big and thick, and fills up the mouth when extended, is called an enlarged tongue (Fig. 2-41). A tongue body that is big and swollen, and when extended, fills up the mouth and oral cavity and cannot be retracted is called an enlarged and swollen tongue (Fig. 2-42).

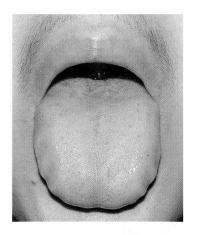

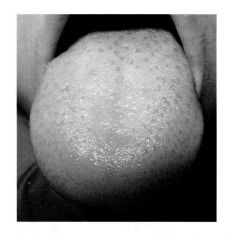

Fig. 2-41 ▲   Fig. 2-42 ▲

Mechanism: It usually results from the stagnation of damp and phlegm, or the invasion of heat and alcohol toxins.

Significance: Stagnation of internal damp and phlegm damp and toxic heat invading upward.

A pale, enlarged tongue with moist coating is usually attributable to insufficiency of spleen and kidney yang with accumulation of the phlegm damp (Fig. 2-43).

A pale enlarged tongue with thick and greasy coating is usually attributable to deficiency of spleen with the internal detention of phlegm-rheum and damp (Fig. 2-44).

A red, swollen tongue with yellow, greasy coating is usually attributable to damp heat in the spleen and stomach, or excess heat in the heart and stomach (Fig. 2-45).

A purple and enlarged tongue is due to upward attack of fire in the heart with alcohol toxin (Fig. 2-46).

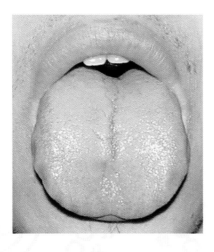

Fig. 2-43 ▲

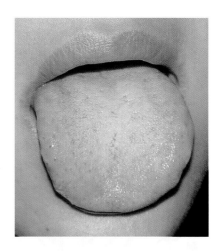

Fig. 2-44 ▲

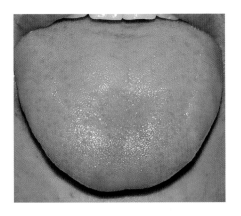

Fig. 2-45 ▲

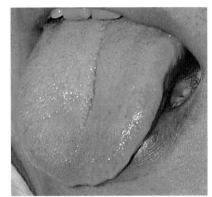

Fig. 2-46 ▲

The enlarged, bluish purple and lusterless tongue accompanied by blue lips, is due to stagnation of blood which is frequently seen in poisoning (Fig. 2-47).

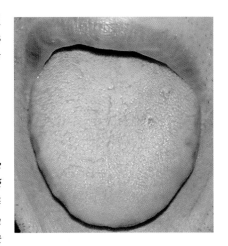

Fig. 2-47 ▲

Guide to Tongue Diagnosis-Differentiating the Shape and Appearance of the Tongue (Biàn Shé Zhǐ Nán-Biàn Shé Zhī Xíng Róng, 辨舌指南·辨舌之形容*)* says *"If the tongue body is swollen enough to fill the mouth, it is usually due to heat in the heart and stomach. A swollen tongue that is red in color primarily suggests excess heat in the heart channel and stagnation of blood. A swollen tongue that is dark purple is often seen in alcohol poisoning or intoxication with drugs. A puffy, bluish purple tongue and lips are frequently seen in poisoning. A thick, purple and enlarged tongue often results from the upward attack of fire in the heart with alcohol toxin, or stagnation of heat caused by drinking cold alcohol."*

THE THIN TONGUE

Features: A tongue smaller and thinner than normal is called a thin tongue (Fig. 2-48).

Mechanism: It is usually caused by deficient qi and blood failing to nourish the tongue, or deficiency of yin fluids, or hyperactivity of fire due to deficiency of yin.

Significance: Dual deficiency of qi and blood or hyperactivity of fire due to yin deficiency.

A pale, thin tongue is usually due to qi and blood deficiency (Fig. 2-49, Fig. 2-50).

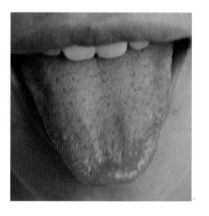

Fig. 2-48 ▲

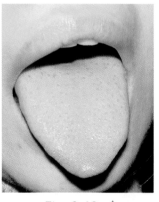

Fig. 2-49 ▲

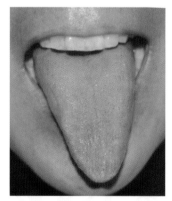

Fig. 2-50 ▲

A tender, red, thin tongue is usually due to insufficient yin in the heart (Fig. 2-51, Fig. 2-52).

A dry, thin tongue that is red or crimson is often due to fire flaring from yin deficiency (Fig. 2-53, Fig. 2-54).

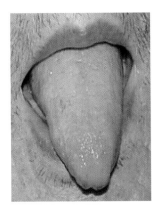

Fig. 2-51 ▲

Fig. 2-52 ▲

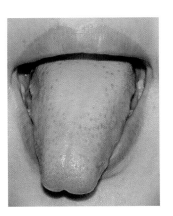

Fig. 2-53 ▲

Fig. 2-54 ▲

THE SPOTTED OR PRICKLED TONGUE

Features: A tongue with red spots is also named a red star tongue or a red spot tongue. It is called this because of the enlarged, multiple and congested fungiform papillae on the surface of the tongue. The big ones are called stars (Fig. 2-55) while the

small ones are called spots (Fig. 2-56). The hyperplastic lingual papillae that protrude like thorns and cause a prickly sensation when they are palpated with finger are found on what is called the prickled tongue (Fig. 2-57). Because these two types of papillae are similar and can be seen at the same time, this type of tongue is usually called a spotted and prickled tongue.

Mechanism: They are primarily caused by excess heat evils, or extreme heat in *zang-fu* organs, or the attack of the blood by epidemic toxins or stagnation of damp heat in the blood. The more serious the heat evils are, the greater the number of spots and prickles will be.

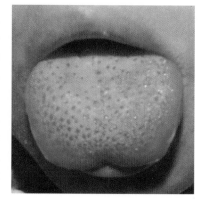

Fig. 2-55 ▲

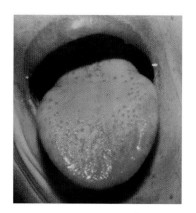

Fig. 2-56 ▲

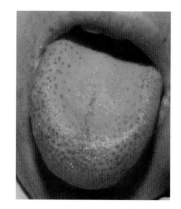

Fig. 2-57 ▲

Significance: Intense heat in the *zang-fu* organs and exuberant heat in the blood level.

⬤   A red tongue with scattered spots and prickles suggests excess heat in the qi level (Fig. 2-58).

⬤   A crimson tongue with prickles spreading over the whole body means heat invading the *ying*-nutrient and blood levels resulting in stagnation of qi and blood (Fig. 2-59).

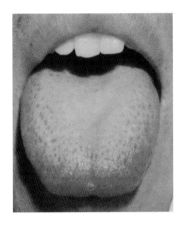

Fig. 2-58 ▲

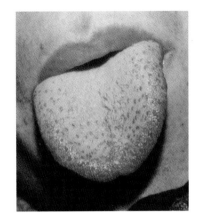

Fig. 2-59 ▲

○ A crimson tongue with dark prickles suggests excess heat evil and the eruption of maculae (Fig. 2-60).

○ Prickles on the tongue tip are due to flaring fire in the heart (Fig. 2-61).

○ Prickles on the sides of the tongue are due to heat in the liver and gallbladder (Fig. 2-62).

○ Prickles in the middle of the tongue are due to heat in the stomach and intestines (Fig. 2-63).

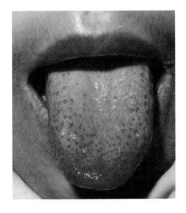

Fig. 2-60 ▲

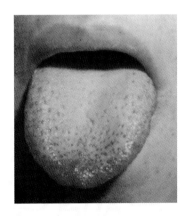

Fig. 2-61 ▲

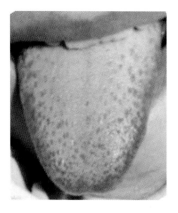

Fig. 2-62 ▲

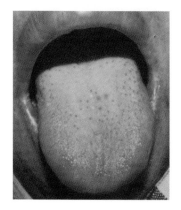

Fig. 2-63 ▲

THE CRACKED TONGUE

Features: If there are cracks of different sizes, depths and shapes in which there is no coating, it is called a cracked tongue (Fig. 2-64).

Mechanism: It is caused by deficient blood failing to manifest on the tongue surface, or injury to the fluids resulting from excess heat, or deficient yin fluids.

Significance: Indicates blood deficiency, excess heat or yin deficiency.

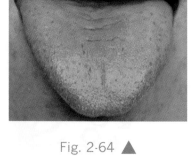

Fig. 2-64 ▲

⬤ A pale tongue with cracks suggests deficiency of blood (Fig. 2-65, Fig. 2-66).

⬤ A dark red tongue with cracks and thick yellow coating on the surface means excess heat in *zang-fu* organs which consumes the fluids (Fig. 2-67).

⬤ A crimson tongue with cracks on the surface but without any coating indicates exhaustion of yin fluids (Fig. 2-68, Fig. 2-69).

A light red tongue with light cracks on the surface which are covered with coating (Fig. 2-70) in a patient with no feelings of being unwell is congenital cracked tongue. These should be distinguished from pathological fissures.

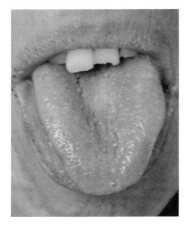

Fig. 2-65 ▲

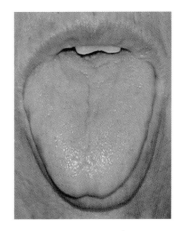

Fig. 2-66 ▲

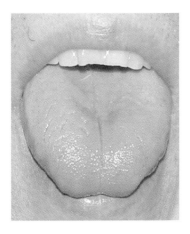

Fig. 2-67 ▲

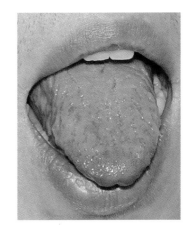

Fig. 2-68 ▲

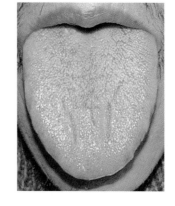

Fig. 2-69 ▲   Fig. 2-70 ▲

THE TEETH MARKED TONGUE

Features: A tongue with teeth marks on its borders is known as teeth marked tongue, and is a result of the pressure of the teeth upon the puffy tongue (Fig. 2-71).

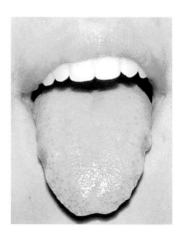

Mechanism: It primarily results from spleen deficiency and excess damp.

Significance: Indicates spleen deficency and water damp stagnation.

⬤ Therefore, a tooth marked tongue often coexists with the enlarged tongue. A pale and moist tongue with teeth marks on its borders usually suggests an excess of cold or cold damp (Fig. 2-72).

Fig. 2-71 ▲

⬤ The red and enlarged tongue filling up the mouth with teeth marks on its margins suggests the stagnation of internal damp heat and phlegm (Fig. 2-73).

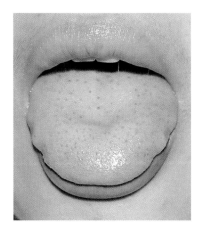

Fig. 2-72 ▲

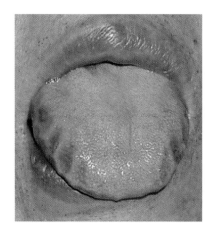

Fig. 2-73 ▲

Section 4
Diagnosing the Condition of the Tongue

The condition of the tongue refers to how the tongue body moves. The normal state of the tongue is to move flexibly, to extend and retract smoothly, and this is a manifestation of smooth channels and collaterals and healthy and vigorous *zang-fu* organs. If the tongue body manifests atrophy, stiffness, deviation, trembling, protruding and wagging, shortness and so on, these are considered pathological conditions.

THE FLACCID TONGUE

Features: A weak tongue is unable to protrude and curl, and is called a flaccid tongue (Fig. 2-74).

Mechanism: It results primarily from the failure of the tongue body to be nourished

due to protracted deficiency of qi and blood, or consumption of yin fluids due to excess heat. The *Spirit Pivot-Channels* says, *"Muscle atrophy results in a weak and flaccid tongue."*

Significance: Indicates both qi and blood deficiency and consumption of fluids due to intense heat.

A flaccid tongue that is pale is qi and blood deficient and is the result of lack of nourishment of the tongue body in chronic disease (Fig. 2-75).

A flaccid tongue that is red with yellow coating is due to injury of the body fluids resulted by consuming of excess heat (Fig. 2-76). Just as *Guide to Differentiating the Tongue* says, *"the abruptly dry and red crimson tongue most likely indicates extremely intense pathogenic heat with impairment of yin fluid."*

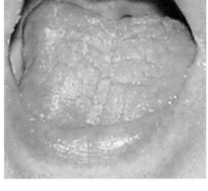

Fig. 2-74 ▲

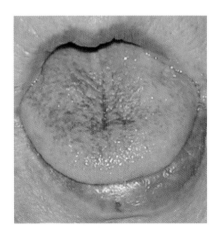

Fig. 2-75 ▲

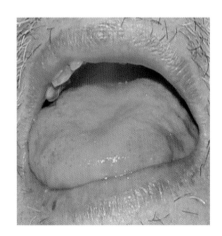

Fig. 2-76 ▲

A glossy and flaccid tongue that is crimson usually belongs to impairment of yin because of intense pathogenic heat in exteriorly contracted diseases, but the

flaring fire is because of deficient yin in diseases due to internal injury (Fig. 2-77).

Fig. 2-77 ▶

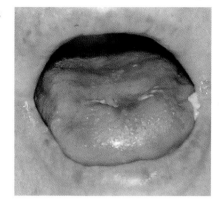

The Stiff Tongue

Features: An inflexible tongue moves with difficulty or is unable to turn. Because the tongue participates in the articulation of the voice, the patient with a stiff tongue frequently suffers from slurred speech (Fig. 2-78).

Mechanism: It primarily results from an attack on the pericardium by excess heat, heat impairment of body fluids due to intense pathogenic heat, or wind phlegm obstructing the channels in the tongue.

Significance:

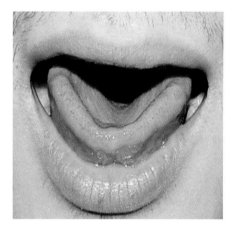

Fig. 2-78 ▲

⬤ A stiff tongue that is a dark red color with high fever is due to an attack on the pericardium by excess heat, and an impairment of the body fluids by intense pathogenic heat (Fig. 2-79).

⬤ An enlarged, stiff tongue with a yellow greasy coating always results from phlegm obstructing the channels (Fig. 2-80).

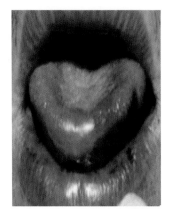

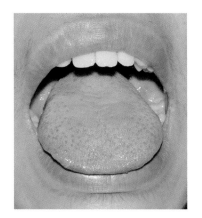

Fig. 2-79 ▲   Fig. 2-80 ▲

Prescriptions Worth a Thousand Gold (*Qiān Jīn Fāng*, 千金方) says, *"For the patient cannot speak with stiff tongue, the disease is in his zang-fu organs."* And *the Guide to Differentiating the Tongue* points out, *"All stiff, red tongues are due to excess heat in the zang-fu organs".*

THE DEVIATED TONGUE

Features: A tongue which turns to one side involuntarily when extended is called the deviated tongue (Fig. 2-81).

Mechanism: In most cases, there is a marked inclination of the anterior half tongue to either the left or the right side. This kind of tongue is primarily due to an obstruction of the collaterals on one side of the tongue body from liver wind stirring in the interior with upward stagnation of phlegm and blood stasis. Since the muscles on the affected side of the tongue are sluggish and weak, the tongue turns to the healthy side when

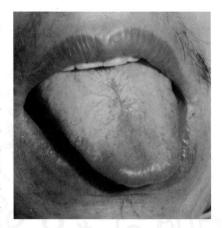

Fig. 2-81 ▲

Atlas of
Tongue
Diagnosis

extended. It often indicates apoplexy or is a premonitory sign of apoplexy, and it often appears simultaneously with a deviated mouth, distorted eyes and hemiplegia.

Significance: Indicates wind stroke or impending wind stroke.

○   If it occurs suddenly and the tongue is red or purple, it is a convulsive condition due to liver wind (Fig. 2-81);

○   When it occurs gradually and the tongue is pale, it is a condition of hemiplegia from wind stroke (Fig. 2-82).

○   Most deviated tongues with dysphasia are a sign of wind stroke (Fig. 2-83).

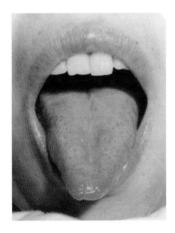
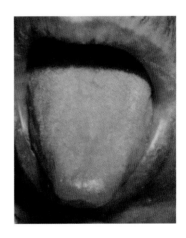

Fig. 2-82 ▲   Fig. 2-83 ▲

The *Guide to Differentiation the Tongue* says, *"If it occurs suddenly and the tongue is red or purple, it is a condition of convulsion due to liver wind, and drugs with the function of calming liver wind should be used. When it occurs gradually and the tongue is pale, it is a condition of hemiplegia or wind stroke. When the deviated tongue appears with symptoms such as a deviated mouth, distorted eyes and hemiplegia, it suggests wind stroke."*

THE TREMBLING TONGUE

Features: It refers to shivering in light diseases and even swaying that can not be controlled by the patient. In serious diseases, when the tongue is not extended it still trembles and is difficult to control.

Mechanism: It primarily results from deficient blood and yin due to malnutrition of the tongue body, or liver wind and yang stirring internally caused by excess heat and ascending hyperactivity of yang. It is always a sign of liver wind stirring internally.

Significance: Liver wind stirring internally. (There is no picture since the trembling tongue cannot be portrayed in a two dimensional picture.)

○ A trembling tongue that is pale is due to internal wind caused by deficient blood.

○ A trembling tongue that is red with little fluid is often due to internal wind caused by deficient yin or liver yang transforming to wind.

○ Trembling in a red or crimson tongue is often due to extreme heat which damages the body fluids and leads to internal wind.

○ It is also seen with alcohol intoxication.

PROTRUDING AND WAGGING TONGUES

Features: A tongue which is extended from the mouth and cannot be retracted immediately is called a protruding tongue (Fig. 2-84). And the tongue that is extended outward and immediately retracted or one that licks the lips and corners of the mouth is called a wagging tongue (Fig. 2-85).

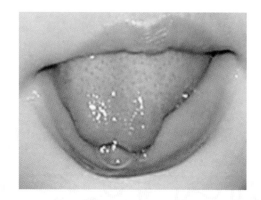

Fig. 2-84 ▲   Fig. 2-85 ▲

Mechanism: It is usually a result of excess heat in the heart and spleen and consumption of the body fluids which leads to a failure to nourish the liver tendons and leads to internal liver wind, or impairment of body fluids and consumption of essence resulting in a failure to nourish the tongue body which causes the tongue to contract. Therefore, patients must stick the tongue out or lick with it in order to extend it.

Significance: Primarily indicates heat in the heart and spleen channels.

● Frequent protrusion of the tongue is usually seen in cases of an attack on the heart by epidemic toxin or exhaustion of the normal qi (Fig. 2-84).

● Wagging tongue is often seen in infants with poor mental development, or is considered to be a sign of wind stroke (Fig. 2-85).

THE SHORTENED TONGUE

Features: A tongue which contracts and shortens, and is unable to be extended even as far as the teeth is called a shortened tongue (Fig. 2-86).

Mechanism: It is usually caused by cold coagulating in the channels and contracture of the tendons resulting from deficient qi and blood, or excess heat impairing the body fluids. It is usually seen simultaneously with a flaccid tongue.

Significance:

● A shortened moist tongue that is a pale or bluish purple is due to cold that has coagulated in channels and caused contracture of the tongue tendons (Fig. 2-87).

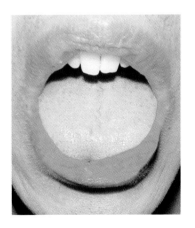

Fig. 2-86 ▲

● A shortened, fat and tender tongue that is pale is due to deficiency of qi and blood or a deficient spleen that fails to nourish the tongue tendons (Fig. 2-88).

● A shortened, dry tongue that is red or crimson in color is due to body fluid impairment due to excess heat which causes the contracture of the tendons and channels (Fig. 2-89).

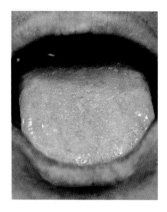

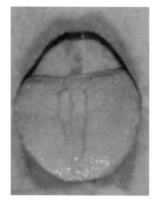

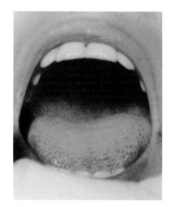

Fig. 2-87 ▲   Fig. 2-88 ▲   Fig. 2-89 ▲

Aside from this, a congenitally shortened frenulum always causes the tongue to curl which is harmless and should be distinguished from the shortened tongue. The *Guide to Differentiating the Tongue* says, *"If the shortened tongue is present at birth, it has no connection to the length of life."* If it occurs with disease, it is in most instances a dangerous symptom.

Section 5
Diagnosing the Sublingual Vessels

Sublingual vessels are the two thick bluish purple vessels that can be seen beside the frenulum of tongue in a normal situation. Their diameter is no more than 2.7 millimeters, and their length is no more than three fifth of the length from tongue tip to the sublingual caruncle. Their color is pale purple and there is no varicosity, contracture, curvature or hyperplasia and they are orderly. Most of them are a single branch and a few of them have two branches (Fig. 2-90).

Fig. 2-90 ▶

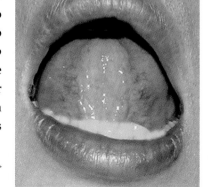

Atlas of
Tongue
Diagnosis

Diagnosing the sublingual vessels means observing changes in their length, state, color or thickness as well as noting any changes in the small vessels below the tongue in order to help diagnose disease.

METHODS OF OBSERVING THE SUBLINGUAL VESSELS

Patients should open their mouth, raise the tongue body upward towards the palate, and touch the tongue tip to the upper palate or to the inside of the front teeth softly keeping the tongue body relaxed so that the sublingual vessels remain composed (Fig. 2-91). The inspector should observe not only changes in the length, thickness, state, size and color of the sublingual vessels or the small vessels nearby, but also any abnormality in varicosity or curvature.

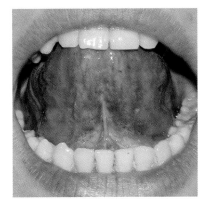

Fig. 2-91 ▲

THE CLINICAL SIGNIFICANCE OF ABNORMAL SUBLINGUAL VESSELS

A pale tongue with shortened, thin sublingual vessels with no nearby vessels primarily suggests insufficient qi and blood failing to fill the vessels (Fig. 2-92). If the vessels become thicker and they turn bluish purple, crimson, crimson purple or dark purple, or there is a network of dark red or purple vessels below the tongue, or the sublingual vessels are stretched and crooked with nodes like purple pearls of unequal size, it is a sign of blood stasis (Fig. 2-93, Fig. 2-94). This is usually due to the stagnation of qi, congealing of cold, depression of heat, accumulation of phlegm, qi deficiency, or yang deficiency. The doctor should analyze these changes and combine them with other symptoms.

Changes in the sublingual vessels occur earlier than changes in the color of the tongue, so observation of the sublingual vessels is an important basis for analyzing the movement of qi and blood, and it they are relatively significant in differentiating between blood deficiency and blood stasis.

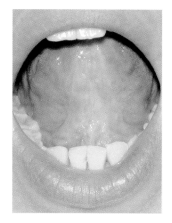

Fig. 2-92 ▲

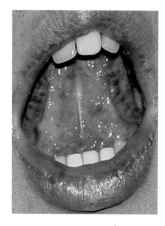

Fig. 2-93 ▲

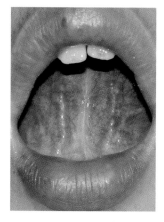

Fig. 2-94 ▲

CHAPTER THREE

Diagnosing The Tongue Coating

The tongue coating is a layer of fur-like substance that comes from the upward fuming of the spleen and stomach qi, and the coagulation stomach fluid on the surface of the tongue. As Zhang Xu-gu (章虚谷) says in *Original Meaning of the Discussion of Cold Damage-Differentiation of the Tongue Coating (Shāng Hán Lùn Běn Zhǐ-Biàn Shé Tāi, 伤寒论本旨 · 辨舌苔)*, *"The tongue coating is made up of stomach qi which rises from the heart and spleen, so a normal person always has a thin coating. It means the stomach qi is vigorous. It is just like the grass that grows in fertile soil."* The abnormal coating is also formed from ascending stomach qi, but it is comprised of a combination of stomach qi and evils which are steamed up together. Just as Zhang Xu-gu says, *"The coating becomes thicker because stomach qi and evils are steamed up in combination. It is just like the grass roots that grow vigorously in dirty and turbid soil."*

The essence of the human body is the qi of the stomach, and the stomach has always been called *"the reservoir of water and food"*. The qi of the five-*zang* and six-*fu* organs all come from the stomach. Changes in the stomach qi can influence the *zang-fu* organs, the qi and blood, and the channels and collaterals. The coating is formed under the steaming action of the stomach qi. Therefore, changes in the tongue coating may reflect diseases of the five-*zang* and the six-*fu* organs. Just as *Simple Exploration of Exterior Diagnosis of Shape and Color* says, *"The coating is formed under the steaming action of the stomach qi. The qi of the five zang and the six fu arises from the stomach. Therefore, we can diagnose cold, heat, deficiency or excess of the five zang."* The significance of observing changes in the coating is as follows: to predict the character of the evil, to detect the location of the disease, to infer the tendency of disease, to judge the sufficiency or insufficiency of the body fluids, to distinguish the exuberance or decline of the evil, to judge whether the disease is advancing or retreating, and to determine whether the prognosis is good or bad.

A normal coating is white in color, evenly distributed and spread thinly over the surface of the tongue, and not too wet and nor too dry. It is a little thicker in the middle and at the root of the tongue. Because the stomach qi of the patient can be strong or weak, the pathogenic evil hot or cold, this accounts for the appearance of different types of pathological tongue coats.

Observation is the main way of inspecting the coating. Touching, feeling, wiping, scraping and other methods should be used to assist the diagnosis when necessary. It is important to take note of changes in the quality and color of the coating.

Section 1
Diagnosing the Quality of the Tongue Coating

Tongue quality refers to the texture and nature of the coating. Aspects often seen in clinic are thickness versus thinness, moistness versus dryness, greasiness versus putridity, how easily it can be removed, and trueness versus falseness of the coat.

THIN AND THICK COATINGS

Features: The "bottom can be seen" or the "bottom cannot be seen" is the standard method for judging the thickness or thinness of the coating. The tongue body (bottom) can be seen indistinctly through a thin coating (Fig. 3-1). The tongue body cannot be seen through a thick coating (Fig. 3-2). Observing the thickness or thinness of the coating is helpful in determining the deepness or shallowness, or the waxing and waning of a disease.

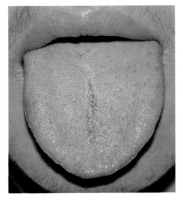

Fig. 3-1 ▲

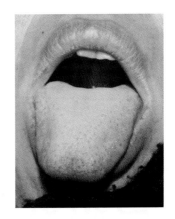

Fig. 3-2 ▲

Mechanism: A thin tongue coating is the appearance of the qi of the stomach which has ascended. A thick tongue coating is caused by pathogenic evil invading upwards.

Significance: Indicates the waxing and waning of evil versus normal qi as well as the depth of pathogenic qi.

⬤ Thin and even coating which is neither too dry nor too wet and is a little thicker in the middle of the tongue is a sign of health (Fig. 3-3). It suggests vigorous stomach qi and an active force in the stomach.

⬤ Thick coating is formed by the retention of damp, phlegm, food and heat evils on the surface of the tongue due to ascension of the stomach qi. It is usually seen in syndromes of phlegm damp, retention of food and interior heat etc. (Fig. 3-4). *Guide to Differentiating the Tongue* says, *"thick and dirty coating indicates rich pathogenic factors."*

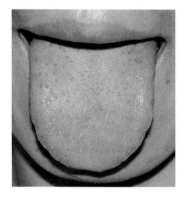

Fig. 3-3 ▲

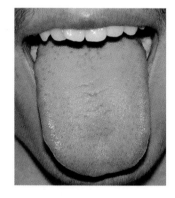

Fig. 3-4 ▲

⬤ In most cases, thick coating suggests an interior syndrome. Thick coating will become more evident when there is retention in the gastrointestinal tract (Fig. 3-5).

⬤ Observing the thickness or thinness of the coating is helpful in predicting the depth of the evil. Generally speaking, when disease is in the exterior, or symptoms are mild and the stomach qi has not yet been injured in an interior disease, the coating will often be thin (Fig. 3-6). A thin coating

suggests an externally contracted exterior syndrome or a mild internal syndrome (Fig. 3-7).

When evils enter the interior, or there is retention of phlegm or food in the gastrointestinal tract, the coating will usually appear on the surface of the middle and root of the tongue (Fig. 3-8).

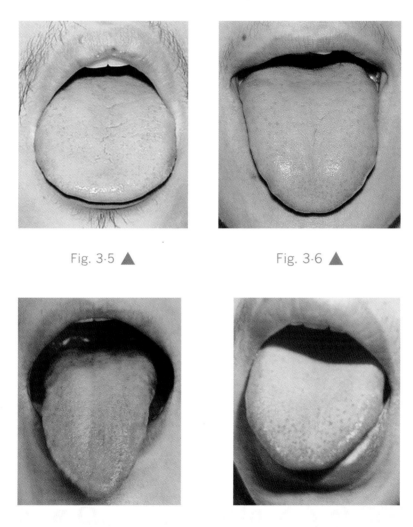

Fig. 3-5 ▲   Fig. 3-6 ▲

Fig. 3-7 ▲   Fig. 3-8 ▲

Observation of transformations in the thickness or thinness of the coating is helpful in distinguishing the waxing and waning of an evil. If a thin coating becomes thick, it indicates that a more vigorous evil has entered the interior from the exterior and that the disease has changed from mild to severe, or that a hidden evil has been exposed and the condition of the patient is deteriorating (Fig. 3-9, Fig. 3-10). When a thick coating recedes and is replaced by a new thin white coating, it is a sign that an evil has been defeated by the normal qi, or that an evil has been cleared and the patient is improving (Fig. 3-11, Fig. 3-12).

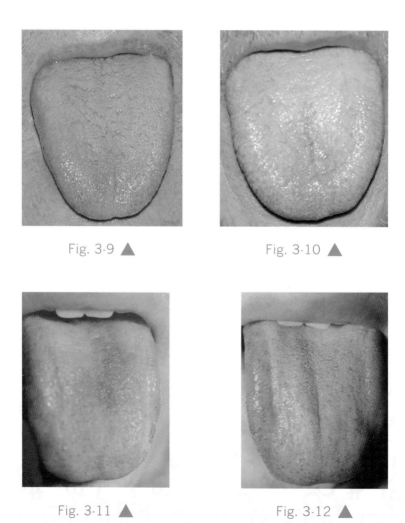

Fig. 3-9 ▲   Fig. 3-10 ▲

Fig. 3-11 ▲   Fig. 3-12 ▲

The transformation of the thickness or thinness of the coating is a slow process. If a thin coating suddenly becomes thicker, this indicates that extreme excess evil has entered the interior quickly (Fig. 3-13, Fig. 3-14). If the coating suddenly clears up and a new coating does not appear, it indicates that the evil has not been defeated by the normal qi or that the stomach qi has suddenly been exhausted (Fig. 3-15, Fig. 3-16).

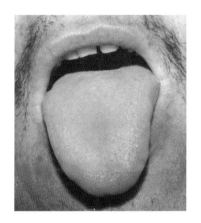

Fig. 3-13 ▲

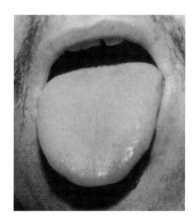

Fig. 3-14 ▲

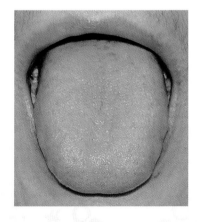

Fig. 3-15 ▲

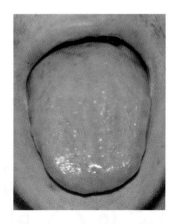

Fig. 3-16 ▲

MOIST AND DRY COATINGS

Features: Moistness and dryness reflect the waxing and waning as well as the distribution of the body fluids. A moist coating with moderate fluid which is neither glossy nor dry is called a moist coating (Fig. 3-17). Fur which looks excessively moist, even to the point of dripping when the tongue is extended, is called glossy coating (Fig. 3-18). Fur which appears dry and lacks fluid, or is even fissured is called dry coating (Fig. 3-19). Dry coating without any fluid on it which might even be rough like sandpaper is called a rough coating (Fig. 3-20).

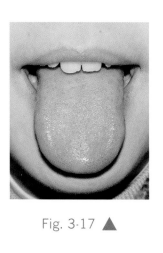

Fig. 3-17 ▲

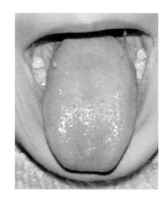

Fig. 3-18 ▲

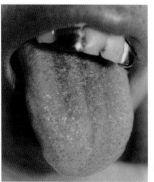

Fig. 3-19 ▲

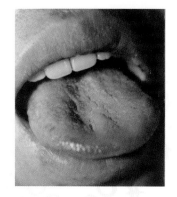

Fig. 3-20 ▲

Atlas of
Tongue
Diagnosis

Mechanism: The moist coat is mostly "stomach fluid" (wèi jīn, 胃津) and "kidney humor" (shèn yè, 肾液) carried upward; The glossy coat is damp collecting on the surface of the tongue; dry, rough coats indicated damage to the body fluids.

Significance: Mainly reflects the waxing and waning of the body fluids as well as the transportation and of the body fluids.

⬤ A moist coating is considered to be normal (Fig. 3-21). It results from the upward distribution of plentiful fluids from the stomach and kidney to the surface of the tongue. A moist coating suggests that the body fluids have not been impaired in diseases such as exterior wind cold, early stage damp, retention of food, and blood stasis (Fig. 3-22).

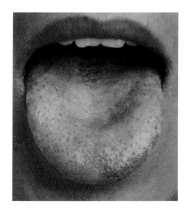

Fig. 3-21 ▲

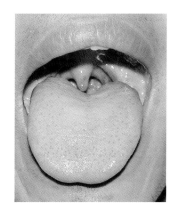

Fig. 3-22 ▲

⬤ Glossy coating is a manifestation of the internal accumulation of water damp evil (Fig. 3-23). It is often seen in phlegm or damp syndromes. It primarily results from an invasion of cold damp into the interior or the retention of cold damp and phlegm due to deficient yang failing to transport and transform water (Fig. 3-24).

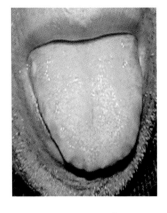

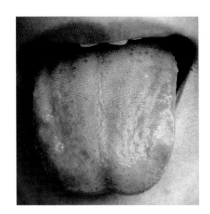

Fig. 3-23 ▲   Fig. 3-24 ▲

⬤ Dry coating is due to injury of the body fluids resulting from high fever, excessive perspiration, excessive vomiting or diarrhea, or depletion of yin due to the overuse of warming and drying herbs (Fig. 3-25). It can also be due to an abnormal distribution of body fluids resulting from the retention of phlegm, blood stasis, obstruction due to the retention of phlegm or blood stasis, or the obstruction of yang which results in a failure to transform water into body fluids that then moisten what is above (Fig. 3-26, Fig. 3-27).

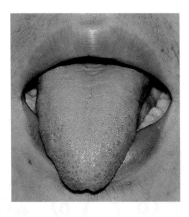

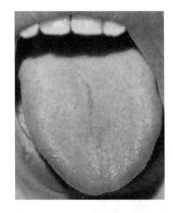

Fig. 3-25 ▲   Fig. 3-26 ▲

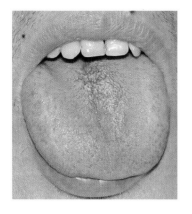

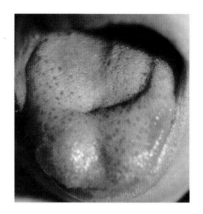

Fig. 3-27 ▲   Fig. 3-28 ▲

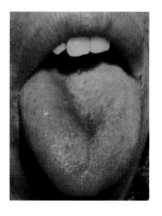

A rough coating usually develops from dry coating. The coating is rough and dry without any fluid on it, and is primarily seen along with serious symptoms that result from excess heat impairing the body fluids (Fig. 3-28). If the coating is rough but not dry, this results primarily from the retention of fetid evils in the middle *jiao* (Fig. 3-29).

The transformation of moist coating into dry coating suggests the consumption of body fluids due to excess heat or the failure to distribute body fluids to the coating. The transformation of dry coating into moist coating indicates the receding of heat and recovery of the body fluids, or the transformation of phlegm evil.

Fig. 3-29 ▲

Guide to Differentiating the Tongue says, "*Moist coatings exists under normal conditions and dry coatings exist under abnormal conditions. Moistness indicates sufficient body fluids and dryness indicates exhaustion of the body fluids*".

Aside from this, *New Methods of Differentiating Syndromes by Examining the Tongue* (*Chá Shé Biàn Zhèng Xīn Fǎ*, 察舌辨证新法) points out, "*Generally speaking, moistness suggests syndromes of damp and dryness suggests syndromes of heat. However, some dry coatings are not due to heat. When dampness enters into the qi level resulting in a failure to produce fluids, a dry coating may be seen. Some moist coatings are not due*

to cold. When warm evil enters the blood, it is a condition of yang evil entering yin and causing the yin to stream upward. Contrary to the syndrome of heat, the coating becomes moist." All of the above show the theories about the formation of moist and dry coating vary respectively.

CURD-LIKE AND GREASY COATINGS

Features: A compact coating that consists of small grain-like bits that merge into larger pieces, is thinner at the margins and thicker in the middle of the tongue surface, sticks tightly to the surface of the tongue and is difficult to scrape off is called a greasy coating (Fig. 3-30). It looks like it is covered with greasy mucus. The looser coating that consists of larger grains and looks like bean curd dregs heaped on the tongue surface, is thick at the margins and in the middle of the tongue surface, and is easily scraped off is called a curd-like coating (Fig. 3-31). A coating that looks like pus and is thick sticky is called the pussy curd-like coating (Fig. 3-32).

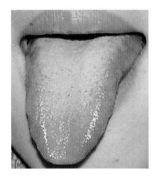
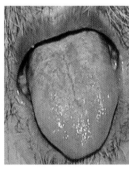
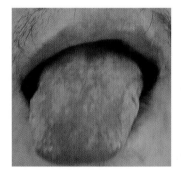

Fig. 3-30 ▲   Fig. 3-31 ▲   Fig. 3-32 ▲

Mechanism: A greasy coating is the result of retention of pathogenic damp and phlegm in the interior and on the tongue due to depression of yang qi. The curd-like coating, on the other hand, usually results from the ascent of stale and turbid substances and pathogens in the stomach that is steamed by excess yang heat. The pussy curd-like coating can usually be seen with interior carbuncles and a combination of toxins and evils. It is a sign of excess evils and serious diseases.

Significance: A greasy coating primarily indicates retention of phlegm and turbid dampness, and secondarily indicates food retention. A curd-like coating primarily indicates food retention and secondarily indicates retention of phlegm and turbid dampness.

    ⬤ A thin and greasy, or greasy but not sticky coating primarily suggests the retention of food, or yang encumbered by accumulated internal damp blocking the qi mechanism (Fig. 3-33).

    ⬤ If it is white, it is due to the retention of turbid phlegm and cold damp which encumbers the yang qi and blocks the qi mechanism (Fig. 3-34).

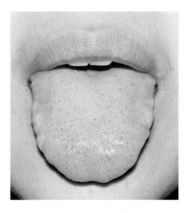

Fig. 3-33 ▲

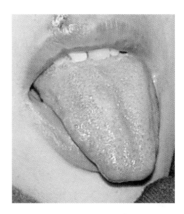

Fig. 3-34 ▲

    ⬤ If the coating is thick, sticky and greasy, and is accompanied by a sweet taste in the mouth, it is due to the rising of accumulated evil and damp heat in the spleen and stomach (Fig. 3-35).

    ⬤ If the coating is yellow, greasy and thick, it is due to the accumulation of phlegm heat evil, damp heat or summerheat damp that obstructs the qi of the *fu* organs (Fig. 3-36, Fig. 3-37).

    ⬤ A curd-like coating results from food retention in the stomach and Intestines or the stagnation of turbid phlegm (Fig. 3-38, Fig. 3-39).

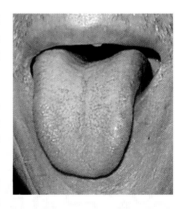

Fig. 3-35 ▲

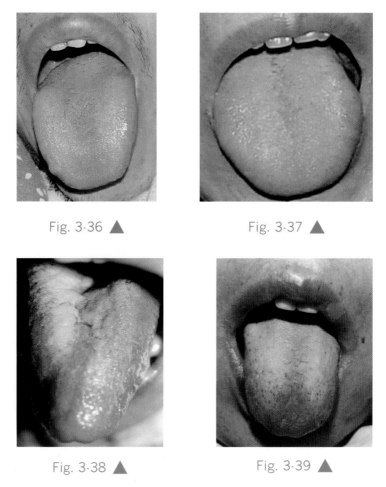

Fig. 3-36 ▲

Fig. 3-37 ▲

Fig. 3-38 ▲

Fig. 3-39 ▲

If a curd-like coating disappears slowly and a new thin white coating appears during the course of a disease, it is a sign that the evil has been defeated by the normal qi and has vanished. If a curd-like coating disappears but no new coating forms, it is a sign of the decline of the stomach qi or of weakened normal qi failing to defeat the evil.

PEELED COATINGS

Features: During the course of a disease, if the tongue coating is fully or

Atlas of
Tongue
Diagnosis

partially peeled to reveal a glossy tongue with no coating, this is called peeling of the coating (Fig. 3-40).

Mechanism: It primarily results from a lack of stomach qi which then fails to steam upward toward the tongue, or the exhaustion of stomach yin resulting failure to moisten the tongue. It is also a sign of deficiency of the whole body.

Significance: In general, the tendency of a coating to peel is a result of impairment of both the stomach qi and the stomach yin.

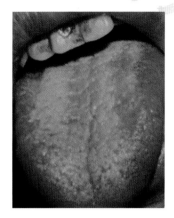

Fig. 3-40 ▲

Peeled coatings can be divided into several types:

○ If the coating is peeled on the front half of the tongue, it is called front peeled coating (Fig. 3-41), and suggests insufficient lung yin.

○ If the coating is peeled in the middle of the tongue, it is called middle peeled coating and primarily indicates deficiency of the spleen and stomach (Fig. 3-42).

○ If the coating is peeled at the root of the tongue, it is called root peeled coating and usually points to exhaustion of the kidney yin (Fig. 3-43).

○ The partial peeling of the coating where there is no coating on the peeled portion is called incomplete peeled coating (Fig. 3-44). It suggests evil excess and yin deficiency.

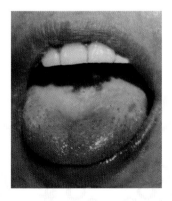

Fig. 3-41 ▲

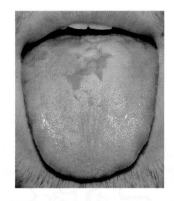

Fig. 3-42 ▲

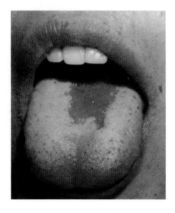

Fig. 3-43 ▲

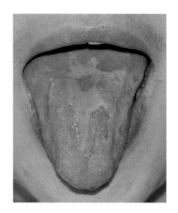

Fig. 3-44 ▲

⬤　If the partial peeling of the coating where have greasy coating on the peeled portion. It primarily results from a deficiency of normal qi which results in a failure to transform turbid phlegm, and the symptoms are more complicated (Fig. 3-45).

⬤　The partially peeled coating where only the center of the tongue surface has a coating is called a chicken heart coating (Fig. 3-46), and it suggests deficiency of qi and blood, especially deficiency of yin blood.

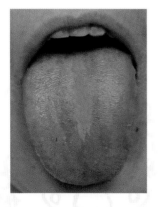

Fig. 3-45 ▲

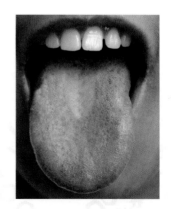

Fig. 3-46 ▲

A tongue without coating which is as smooth as a mirror is called a mirror tongue or a bare tongue (Fig. 3-47) and suggests the exhaustion of yin fluid in the kidney and stomach. It is a sign of a deficiency of active qi in the stomach and is a part of serious syndromes that result from a deficiency of yin.

The coating which is peeled irregularly, protrudes from the margins, has a clear boundary and looks like a map with the locations being transferred from place to place is sometimes called a geographic tongue (Fig. 3-48). It is usually seen in children and is connected to congenital deficiency of yin.

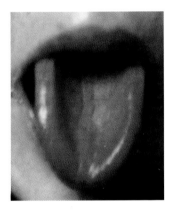

Fig. 3-47 ▲

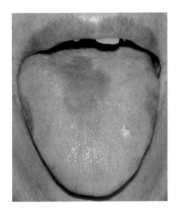

Fig. 3-48 ▲

If the peeled portion is somewhat rough and covered with newly produced particles on which lingual mamillary papillae can be seen, it is called peeled-type coating (Fig. 3-49). It is primarily a sign of deficient blood, insufficient qi and blood, or discontinuation of the production of qi and blood because of chronic disease.

In general, observation of the waxing and waning of exfoliation is helpful in distinguishing the existence or loss of the stomach qi and stomach yin, as a reflection of the exuberance or decline of the normal qi, and in determining the prognosis for the disease. A change from the presence of coating to an absence

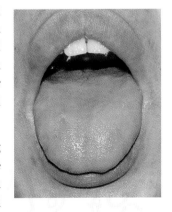

Fig. 3-49 ▲

of coating is a manifestation of a deficiency of qi and yin in the stomach and a gradual weakening of the normal qi. On the contrary, the regeneration of a thin, white coating after it has stripped off is regarded as favorable sign of conquest of the pathogens by the normal qi and a gradual recovery of the stomach qi.

EVEN AND UNEVEN COATINGS

Features: A coating which is evenly spread all over the surface of the tongue is called an even coating (Fig. 3-50). If the coating is only found on some parts of tongue surface, it is called an uneven coating (Fig. 3-51). The uneven coating may be on the front, rear, left or right portions of the tongue.

Mechanism: Even coating is due to the spreading of evil, or to the retention of damp phlegm in diseases. For the uneven coating, the evenness of the coating on a particular part suggests the accumulation and retention of evil in the corresponding *zang-fu* organs.

Significance:

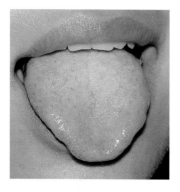
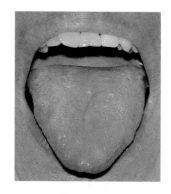

Fig. 3-50 ▲

Fig. 3-51 ▲

An uneven coating on the outer part of the tongue (near the tip) is due to evil in the interior but not deep in the interior, and also to stomach qi deficiency (Fig. 3-52).

⬤ An uneven coating on the inner part of the tongue (near the root) is due to the vanishing of exterior evil but heavy food retention in the stomach (Fig. 3-53).

⬤ An uneven coating found only in the middle of the tongue is due to the retention of phlegm and food in the middle *jiao* (Fig. 3-54).

⬤ An even coating on one side, either the left or the right, usually suggests damp heat evil in the liver and gallbladder (Fig. 3-55).

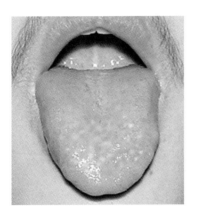

Fig. 3-52 ▲

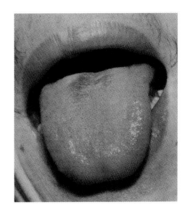

Fig. 3-53 ▲

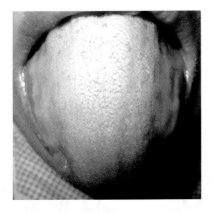

Fig. 3-54 ▲

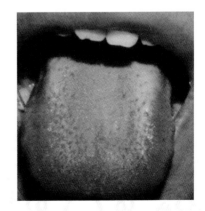

Fig. 3-55 ▲

An uneven coating should be distinguished from a peeled coating. The former is a pathological phenomenon of coating distribution; the latter is a case where the original coating peeled away resulting in an uneven coating. A thicker coating on one side usually results from tooth loss and reduced friction, and should be differentiated from a pathological uneven coating.

TRUE AND FALSE COATINGS

Features: True coating refers to the sturdy coating that closely adheres to the tongue body and is difficult to scraping off. Signs of the coating remain after being scraped off, and the quality of the tongue is not exposed. It looks like the coating is growing out of the tongue body. It is also called a rooted coating (Fig. 3-56). A false coating does not closely adhere to the tongue body and is easy to scrape off. It looks like it has been placed on the tongue body. The quality of the tongue is therefore smooth and clear after the coating has been scraped off. It is also called an unrooted coating (Fig. 3-57).

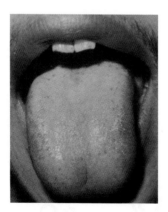

Fig. 3-56 ▲

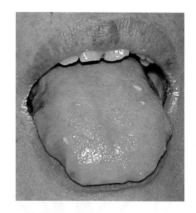

Fig. 3-57 ▲

Mechanism: The true coating is formed from the upper accumulation on the tongue of evils such as turbid food steamed by the spleen and stomach qi. The coating is rooted, so it cannot be separated from the tongue body. The false coating

is due to a deficiency of stomach qi which leads to the failure to produce a new coating, but the old coating slowly breaks away from the tongue body and floats on the surface of the tongue. The coating therefore has no root and leaves behind filth after being scraped off.

Significance: To inspect whether the coating is true or false, it is important to judge the gravity of the diseases and the likelihood of a good prognosis. The thick, true coating that appears in the early and middle stages of a disease suggests excess stomach qi that is jammed and a disease of greater severity. A true coating is also seen in cases of chronic disease and indicates that there is stomach qi remaining. A false coating appears during the course of a disease and is suggestive of deficient stomach qi failing to move upward, and it is a sign of a dangerous disease. When a layer of thick, unrooted coating floating on the surface of the tongue has a thin newly produced coating beneath it after being scraped off, this is a sign of recovery.

Section 2
Diagnosing the Color of the Coating

The colors of the tongue coating are divided into white, yellow, gray and black. They may occur alone or in combination.

WHITE COATINGS

Features: A coating which adheres to the surface of the tongue and is white is called a white coating (Fig. 3-58). It can be divided into thick white and thin white. A thin white coating is one through which the tongue body can be seen (Fig. 3-59). A thick white coating is one through which the body of the tongue cannot be seen (Fig. 3-60).

Mechanism: White is the natural color of the coating. It is a sign of a normal condition, and can usually be seen in exterior syndrome diseases including cold syndromes, damp syndromes and heat syndromes. The other colors are transformations from a white coating.

Significance:

A thin, white, moist coating may be present under normal conditions or can also suggest the beginning of an exterior syndrome, a light or shallow interior syndrome, or interior cold resulting from deficient yang (Fig. 3-61).

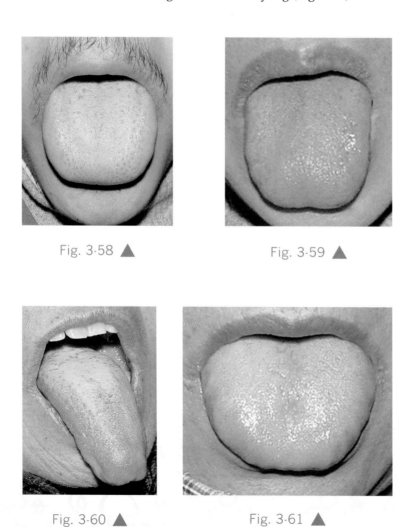

Fig. 3-58 ▲

Fig. 3-59 ▲

Fig. 3-60 ▲

Fig. 3-61 ▲

The thin, white, glossy coating is primarily due to exterior cold damp, or the internal retention of water damp caused by deficient spleen and kidney yang (Fig. 3-62).

A thin, white, dry coating is usually due to exterior wind heat (Fig. 3-63).

A white, thick, greasy coating often results from the internal retention of turbid damp and phlegm caused by unactivated central yang, or the retention of food in the stomach and intestines (Fig. 3-64).

A thick, white, dry coating indicates the internal accumulation of phlegm and damp heat (Fig. 3-65).

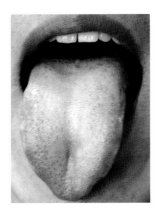

Fig. 3-62 ▲

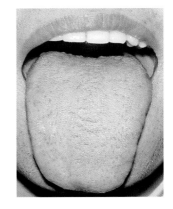

Fig. 3-63 ▲

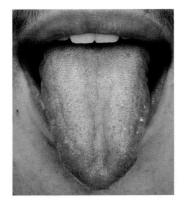

Fig. 3-64 ▲

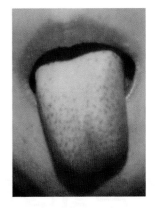

Fig. 3-65 ▲

A white coating spreading over the tongue that looks like heaps of powder, but does not feel dry to the touch, is called a powder-like coating, and is a result of the combination of filthy and turbid damp combined with heat toxin (Fig. 3-66).

It is often seen in epidemics and abscesses of the internal organs. A white, dry coating that resembles sand and feels rough to the touch suggests that the body fluids have been damaged by dry heat and the exhaustion of yin fluid (Fig. 3-67).

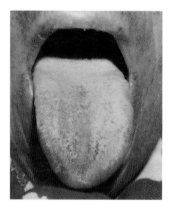

Fig. 3-66 ▲

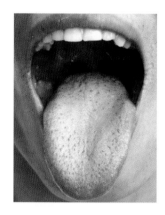

Fig. 3-67 ▲

YELLOW COATINGS

Features: A coating that adheres to the surface of the tongue and is yellow in color is called a yellow coating (Fig. 3-68). It can be divided into light yellow, dark yellow and burned yellow coatings. A light yellow coating, also called a slightly yellow coating, refers to a yellow coating that is light in color (Fig. 3-69). A dark yellow coating, also called a normal yellow coating, refers to a coating that is thick and yellow in color (Fig. 3-70). A burned yellow coating is called an old yellow coating, and refers to a tongue coating which appears yellowish black (Fig. 3-71).

Mechanism: A yellow coating primarily results from the movement of heat

Atlas of
Tongue
Diagnosis

evil or pathological evil to the interior where it transforms into heat. Evil heat fumes upward and scorches the tongue. In general, the amount of yellow in the coating is related to the degree of heat. The deeper the yellow is, the more intense the pathogenic heat will be. A light yellow coating suggests shallow heat while a dark yellow coating suggests deep heat, and a burned yellow coating suggests excess heat. A yellow coating is primarily distributed on the middle of the tongue, but can also spread over the whole tongue. It usually appears with a red or crimson tongue. The quality of a yellow coating can be thick or thin, moist or dry, or greasy.

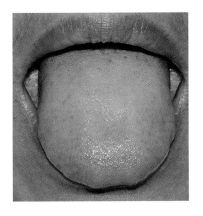

Fig. 3·68 ▲

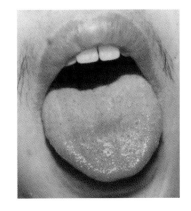

Fig. 3·69 ▲

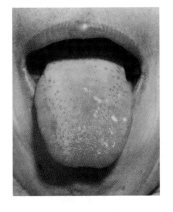

Fig. 3·70 ▲

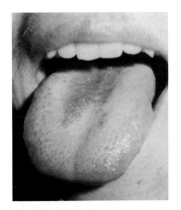

Fig. 3·71 ▲

A change in the color of the coating from white to yellow, or to a combination of white and yellow, suggests that exterior evils have penetrated into the interior and produced heat, or that the stage of disease is one where there is a combination of exterior and interior syndromes. For this reason, *Guide to Cold Damage* says, *"a white coating indicates exterior syndromes while a yellow coating indicates interior syndromes. Taiyang controls the exterior while yangming controls the interior. Therefore, a yellow coating suggests interior syndromes in the yangming. In externally contracted diseases, a white coating means the disease is in the exterior. A yellowish white coating means the disease is partially in the interior and partially in the exterior. If the coating is purely yellow without any white, it is a sign that all of the evils are in the interior."*

Significance: The light yellow coating suggests shallow heat syndrome, while the dark yellow coating suggests deep heat syndrome, and the burned yellow coating suggests extreme heat syndrome.

⬤ A light yellow, thin coating indicates invasion by external wind heat or wind cold that has stagnated and transformed into heat in the interior (Fig. 3-72).

⬤ A dark yellow coating suggests internal heat holding damp, phlegm which has transformed into heat or food that has accumulated and become rotten from heat (Fig. 3-73).

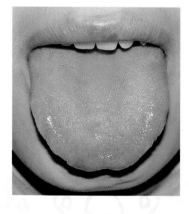

Fig. 3-72 ▲

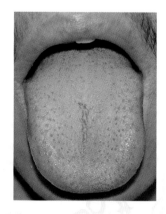

Fig. 3-73 ▲

Atlas of
Tongue
Diagnosis

Burned yellow coating results from damage to the body fluids due to internal heat or dryness bind causing excess syndromes in the *fu* organs (Fig. 3-74).

A yellow slippery coating is so named because the coating is moist, slippery and light yellow in color with a lot of fluid on the tongue surface (Fig. 3-75). It primarily results from constitutional yang deficiency and cold damp, or from the chronic accumulation of phlegm transforming to heat, or the reinvasion of damp heat evil in a body with insufficient qi and blood.

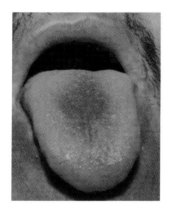
Fig. 3-74 ▲

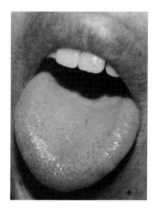
Fig. 3-75 ▲

If the color of the coating is yellow and the quality of the coating is greasy, it is called a yellow greasy coating (Fig. 3-76). It suggests the internal accumulation of damp heat or phlegm heat, or the accumulation of food which turns rotten.

If the quality of a blackish yellow coating is sticky and greasy, it is called a moldy soy sauce coating (Fig. 3-77). It is usually due to turbid damp and undigested food which has been accumulating for a long time that transforms to heat, and the filthy turbidity is steamed upward to the surface of the tongue. It also can be seen in the syndromes where damp heat is holding phlegm.

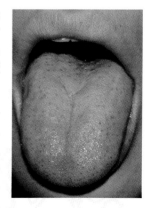
Fig. 3-76 ▲

A coating that is dry and yellow, or one that is dry and stiff with large, rough particles that is rough to the touch, is called a rough yellow coating (Fig. 3-78). A dry yellow coating with fissures like petals in the middle is called a yellow petal coating (Fig. 3-79). A coating that is a combination of yellow and black that looks like burnt rice crust is called a burned yellow coating (Fig. 3-80). Both suggest damage to body fluids by heat evil and syndromes of dryness bind with excess in the *fu*.

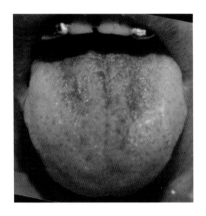

Fig. 3-77 ▲

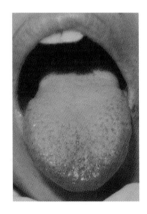

Fig. 3-78 ▲

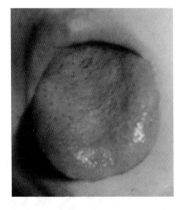

Fig. 3-79 ▲

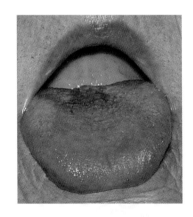

Fig. 3-80 ▲

Atlas of
Tongue
Diagnosis

GRAY AND BLACK COATINGS

Features: A gray coating means that the coating is a light black color (Fig. 3-81). A black coating is so named because the coating is deep gray in color (Fig. 3-82). The only difference between a gray coating and a black coating is the depth of the color. For this reason, it is called a grayish black coating.

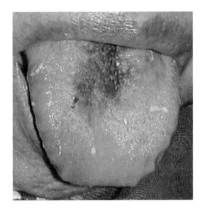

Fig. 3-81 ▲   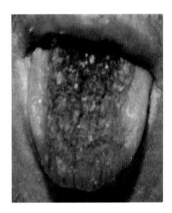 Fig. 3-82 ▲

Mechanism: It primarily transforms from a white or yellow coating. It often appears after a disease has been present for a period of time and then develops further. The grayish black coating might be seen in cold damp disease or in diseases of a hot nature. It results primarily from the excess internal yin cold and heat.

A black coating usually appears in the critical stages of a disease and indicates a severe syndrome of heat or cold. The deeper the color of the coating show, the more severe the disease would be. As *Ao's Record of the Golden Mirror on Cold Damage* says, *"a black coating indicates that fire brightness has been restrained by water. No patient with a black coating can be cured."* The classic also says, *"No patient with a black coating like black lacquer will survive."* The grayish black coating does not absolutely suggest that the case is critical. It can also suggest that the disease is shallow with no obvious symptoms. It can also be caused by too much smoking.

Significance: Indicates yang deficiency and coldness flourishing, or exhaustion of body fluid caused by extreme heat. The moistness or dryness of a coating is an important index for the clinical doctor to use in judging whether the grayish black coating results from cold or heat.

⬤ In diseases of cold damp, the grayish black coating is primarily transformed from a white coating. It will be moist with a lot of fluid on the surface (Fig. 3-83).

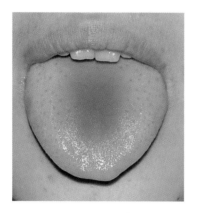

Fig. 3-83 ▲

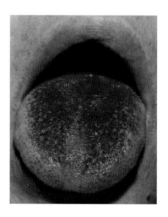

Fig. 3-84 ▲

⬤ The grayish black coating is usually transformed from a yellow coating in cases of diseases of a hot nature. It will be dry with no fluid on the surface (Fig. 3-84).

⬤ A white, greasy coating on the margins and tip of the tongue with a grayish blackcoating in the middle and at the root, and moist tongue body, suggests yang deficiency with vigorous internal cold damp, or the retention and accumulation of phlegm (Fig. 3-85).

⬤ A yellow, greasy coating on the tip and

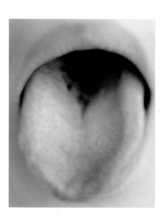

Fig. 3-85 ▲

margins of the tongue with a grayish black coating in the middle suggests internal obstruction by damp heat which has over the course of time failed to transform (Fig. 3-86).

A dry burned black coating, whether in cases of externally contracted or internal disease, is a manifestation of extreme heat and exhaustion of the body fluids (Fig. 3-87).

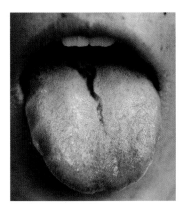

Fig. 3-86 ▲

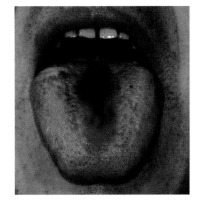

Fig. 3-87 ▲

CHAPTER FOUR

The Clinical Significance and Use of Tongue Diagnosis

Methods for Clinical Examination of the Tongue (*Lín Zhèng Yàn Shé Fǎ*, 临症验舌法) points out, "*...of all internal and external syndromes, there is not one that will not present on the tongue...if deficiency and excess are distinguished according to the tongue, how can they not be clear; if yin and yang are distinguished according to the tongue, how can there be an error; if the zang-fu organs are distinguished according to the tongue and a fitting formula given, how can the location of the disease or the prescription be mistaken? Only the tongue can be depended upon when the disease is severe and difficult to differentiate, or when there are no symptoms to refer to and no pulse to be palpated. The diseases of females and children often yield no information in response to auscultation or olfaction, or no answers to inquiry, and only changes in the tongue can be relied upon.*" It is shown then that the significance of tongue diagnosis is not only universal, but also objective and accurate. The methods of tongue diagnosis are simple and convenient. Therefore, it has become a conventional means of and an important basis for differentiation in Chinese medicine.

Section 1
The Clinical Significance of Tongue Diagnosis

Changes in the tongue reflect the state of an illness objectively and exactly. They can be regarded as an important basis for diagnosing disease, for understanding the development of and changes in the state of an illness, and for differentiation.

JUDGING THE EXUBERANCE OR DECLINE OF PATHOGENIC AND NORMAL QI

The exuberance or decline of normal qi and pathogenic qi manifests on the tongue. A tongue that is full of vitality suggests sufficient normal qi while a lack of vitality suggests insufficient normal qi. A soft, flexible tongue that is light red in color with a thin, white, moist coating indicates sufficient normal qi, the normal movement of qi and blood, and uninjured body fluids. A tongue that is pale usually results from the deficiency of both qi and blood. A dry tongue and coating is due to the impairment of body fluids. A rooted coating means there is sufficient stomach qi while the unrooted or completely peeled coating is usually caused by the decline of stomach qi. A thick coating suggests flourishing pathogenic qi while a thin coating suggests pathogenic qi that is in decline.

DISTINGUISHING THE NATURE OF PATHOGENIC EVIL

Evils of different natures will cause different changes in the tongue. In general, thin, white coatings result primarily from externally contracted wind cold while thin, yellow coatings often result from externally contracted wind heat. A fat tongue with a greasy coating is usually due to the retention of cold damp. A red tongue with a dry coating is always due to an attack by dry evil. The flourishing of internal fire heat often results in a red tongue with a dry, yellow coating. The internal retention of phlegm turbidity usually leads to a sticky, greasy coating. A glossy coating with a lot of fluid on the surface is primarily caused by the retention of water phlegm. A rough and curd-like coating indicates food retention. Aside from the above, sunken, round, red spots on the tongue body might be seen in patients with parasitic diseases. Dark purple spots on the tongue body are primarily a result of blood stasis. The tongue may take on a bluish hue when people are intoxicated. In conclusion, all evils including pathogenic wind, cold, heat, damp, dryness, fire, phlegm, water, food, blood stasis and parasites can be identified based on changes in the tongue.

DISTINGUISHING THE LOCATION AND DEPTH OF DISEASE

Changes in the location of a disease can be reflected in the tongue. The thickness or thinness of the coating and changes in the tongue body can reflect the depth of the location as well as the severity of the disease. Because different areas of the tongue correspond to different *zang-fu* organs, these areas can reflect pathological changes in the various *zang-fu* organs. In general, light and shallow diseases may cause changes in the tongue coating while deeper and more severe diseases may result in simultaneous changes in both the tongue coating and quality. For example, a thin, white coating suggests that the disease is in its initial stages. The disease is shallow and it is considered to be an exterior syndrome. But a thick, yellow coating and red tongue suggest that the disease is severe, that there is excess heat in the qi level, and that it is an interior syndrome. A crimson tongue indicates that the evils have entered the *ying*-nutrient level. A deep crimson or dark purple tongue with little or no coating means that evil has entered the blood level. All of the above show that the depth of the location of the disease can be reflected by different changes in the tongue. The tongue also can reflect the abnormal functioning of the *zang-fu* organs in diseases that are caused by internal injury. In general, prickles on a red tongue tip are due to flourishing heat evil in the heart; red on the sides of tongue is due to heat in the liver and gallbladder. A white, thick, greasy coating primarily indicates that the spleen is failing to transport and transform nutrients and that there is retention of damp in the interior. This is seen in diseases such as damp turbidity and phlegm. A yellow, thick, greasy coating in the middle of the tongue is primarily due to damp heat in the spleen and stomach. The trembling tongue body often results from up wind stirring in the liver. A deviated tongue body is usually the result of or a sign of wind stroke.

PREDICTING THE COURSE OF DISEASE

By observing the dynamic appearance of the tongue, it is possible to follow the development of disease as well as its tendency to advance or recede. For example, a coating that goes from white to yellow, from yellow to grayish black, from thin to thick, or from moist to dry is usually due to the transfer of evil from the exterior to the interior, a change in the severity in the disease from light to severe, from cold to heat, or the impairment and exhaustion of body fluids by the heat evils flourishing in the interior. It shows the deterioration from a disease. On the contrary, a change in the Colour from yellow to white, from thick to thin, or from dry to moist is primarily due to the slow withdrawal of evil and the production of new body fluids. It shows the recovery from a disease. A sudden increase or decrease in the amount of coating usually results from abrupt changes in a disease. An immediate change in the coating from thin to thick is a sign of evils entering the interior rapidly. But the abrupt withdrawal of a thick coating on the whole tongue surface is due to excess evils that are flourishing and a deficiency of the normal qi, or a violent exhaustion of the stomach qi. Both of these signs are serious. If the

color of the tongue color goes from light red to red, crimson or crimson purple, or there are prickles and fissures on the tongue surface, it suggests that the heat evil has entered the *ying*-nutrient and blood levels and will tend to injure the yin and result in blood stasis. If the tongue color turns from light red to pale, or to pale purple, or there are teeth marks on the margins of a fat, tender tongue body, this is due to injured yang and the flourishing of internal cold. It is a sign that the evils have entered the interior from the exterior and that the disease has changed from light to severe. It shows the deterioration from a disease.

Estimating the Prognosis for a Disease

If the tongue vitality appears vigorous, there is coating on the surface of the tongue, and the movement of the tongue is normal. It is a condition that evil is not flourishing, the normal qi is uninjured, and the stomach qi is not exhausted. It shows that the prognosis is good. A withered tongue texture with an unrooted coating and abnormal movement indicates a deficiency of normal qi and the exhaustion of stomach qi. It shows that a disease is severe.

Section 2
Clinical Application of Tongue Diagnosis

Changes in the tongue vary with changes in the disease condition. Tongue diagnosis is widely used and plays an important role in diagnosing and treating various diseases.

Application Of Tongue Diagnosis In The Diagnosis And Treatment Of Warm Disease

The cause of warm disease is mainly heat evil. Symptoms of this type of disease include heat signs. Particular attention must be paid to the changes in the disease

since acute externally contracted warm diseases, which result in fever, can easily dry the person out causing yin damage. Warm disease encompasses wind heat, spring heat, summer heat, dry heat, and infections of the face, diphtheria, scarlet fever, and summer dryness epidemics. Warm disease is similar to many diseases that are characterized by fever. These include acute infectious diseases such as influenza, encephalitis B, epidemic hemorrhagic fever, measles, rubella, infectious mononucleosis, lobar pneumonia, viral pneumonia, acute bronchitis, suppurative tonsillitis, septicemia, septic shock, adult respiratory asthma, and other febrile diseases such as heatstroke, heat apoplexy, pseudo summer fever, acute leukemia, acute rheumatic fever, etc[1].

Ye Tian-shi (叶天士), a physician during the *Qing* Dynasty, stressed the important functions and guiding principles of tongue diagnosis in his work *Discourse on Externally Contracted Warm Heat* (*Wài Gǎn Wēn Rè Piān*, 外感温热篇) thereby creating the syndrome differentiation system referred to as the four levels (*wei*-defense, qi, *ying*-nutrition, *xue*-blood). The utilization of tongue diagnosis in the differentiation of warm disease clinically identifies the type of evil from the color, luster, shape and the condition of the tongue body, and the character of the tongue coating including the color and dryness or moistness of the coating. Information gathered from the tongue helps to differentiate the type of syndrome, judge the amount of fluid depletion, and determine a prognosis, thereby creating a basis for treatment.

1. Exploring the Nature of Pathogenic Evil and Determining the Location of Disease by Observing the Tongue Coating

Du[2] believed that during the onset of warm disease, the course and development of the disease should be considered. Changes in tongue texture and tongue coating reflect the progress of a warm disease. Warm diseases are often acute with a dramatic onset and are typically serious in nature. Generally speaking, the deeper the tongue color, the deeper and more critical the disease is. The progression of the change in the color of the tongue coating is often as follows: white to yellow to gray to black. This means that the externally contracted evils are changing from light to severe, the condition from slight to serious, the level of penetration of the disease from shallow to deep. If the coating is thin, the condition is slight. If the tongue coating is thick, then the condition is more serious. The moistness of the tongue indicates whether fluid injury has occurred. Dryness indicates fluid injury. Song[3] concluded that by

Atlas of
Tongue
Diagnosis

examining and differentiating the tongue, it was possible to determine whether the disease was located in the *wei*-defense, qi, *ying*-nutrient or *xue*-blood level. He also created a method of determining the mechanism and prognosis for a disease in order to develop and pass on Ye Tian-shi's ideas about febrile disease by researching the statements of Ye Tian-shi. Liu[4] believed that a thick and greasy coating was an important basis for diagnosing damp warm diseases when summing up the experience of differentiating damp warm disease through tongue diagnosis. Moreover, a sticky, greasy coating indicates damp heat and stagnation, and the obstruction of turbid evil.

2. Differentiating Tongue Color to Decide on the Level (*Wei*-defense, Qi, *Ying*-nutrient, *Xue*-blood) and Seriousness of the Disease

Du[2] believed that if the tongue coating changes, the tongue color will also change. If the disease has progressed and becomes more serious, then the level of the disease is deeper. This also means the disease has progressed from the *wei*-defense or qi level to the *ying*-nutrient or *xue*-blood level. As far as tongue color is concerned, the deeper the color, the deeper the evil. A red tongue indicates that heat has entered the *ying*-nutrient level whereas a crimson tongue indicates that the evil has gone deeper (two-thirds of the way) into the *ying*-nutrient level. A purple tongue indicates that heat evil has entered the *xue*-blood level. By researching Ye's theories, Zhang[5] came to believe that a crimson tongue is the key characteristic of a warm disease and indicates that the evil has entered the *ying*-nutrient and xue-blood levels. A crimson tongue indicates heat in the *ying*-nutrient level along with dryness, and a purple and crimson tongue indicates blood stasis.

3. Supervising Clinical Syndrome Differentiation and Treatment According to the Appearance of the Tongue

Tongue diagnosis not only provides a basis for syndrome differentiation, but is also helpful in determining an appropriate prescription for consumption by the patient. Hung[6] divides warm disease into eleven categories according to the combination of tongue diagnosis with the four other examination methods. He offers key points in syndrome differentiation for the tongue diagnosis of warm disease. By observing the tongue body, the rise and fall of qi, blood, yin and yang can be determined, the excess, deficient, cold or hot nature of an illness can be identified, and the location of and prognosis for disease can be speculated upon. In seasonal warm diseases caused by externally contracted pathogenic

factors, a red or crimson tongue indicates that the evil heat had moved to the interior. A red prickly tongue with erosions or ulcers in the mouth and on the tongue suggests abundant toxic heat obstructing the interior. A yellow tongue is a manifestation of damp heat in the liver and gallbladder channel with bile overflowing. A thin tongue with fissures suggests yin deficiency due to excess heat evil. A crimson and purple dark tongue indicates that heat evil had already entered the *ying*-nutrient and *xue*-blood levels causing depletion of yin and yang. A swollen tongue that is crimson and purple and moves with difficulty was a manifestation of pericardium invaded by toxic heat. By observing the tongue coating, the location of illness in a particular *zang-fu* organs can be determined. A change in the color of the coating from white to yellow and then to black shows that heat evil has moved from a more superficial level to the interior. When a coating turns from moist to dry, it means that excess heat is damaging the fluids. If a thick, yellow coating, or even a burned black color appears, the pathology is heat evil entering a *fu* organ and fighting with the dregs in the stomach and intestine causing obstruction of the qi of these *fu*. The pathology of a yellow greasy coating is usually accumulation of damp heat or phlegm heat in the interior. Symptoms of bitter taste in the mouth, foul breath and glossalgia are the primary indications for heat evil accumulating in stomach and intestines, damp heat in the liver and gallbladder channels, and excess heat in the heart channel. Judging whether an illness is excess or deficient, or cold or hot by observing the shape of the tongue body is the basis for determining how to expel the heat. Observing the tongue coating to discern the functioning of the stomach and intestines is important in determining whether to purge the heat or not; the taste in the mouth is a standard reference in determining whether to clear and drain fire.

APPLICATION OF TONGUE DIAGNOSIS IN THE DIAGNOSIS AND TREATMENT OF CARDIO-CEREBRAL VASCULAR DISEASES

Chinese medicine believes *"the heart opens into the tongue"*, they are closely related in physiology and pathology. Recent research has found that changes in the appearance of the tongue can sensitively and promptly reflect the functional condition of the cardiovascular system, and that they are significant in the treatment and diagnosis of and the prognosis for cardiovascular disease.

1. Hypertension

As a basic disease of the cardio-cerebral vascular system, hypertension can lead to coronary heart disease, apoplexy and heart failure; high blood pressure increases the risk of mortality. It also increases the risk of kidney disease as well as causes pathological changes in the aorta and peripheral arteries.

Yang[7] discovered that the occurrence of this disease is closely related to changes in the tongue body and coating by observing the appearance of the tongues of 100 patients with hypertension. For example, patients who showed evidence of a pattern of exuberant liver fire presented with a red tongue. Patients with a pattern reflective of hyperactivity of yang due to yin deficiency displayed a red or crimson tongue. Patients with a pattern of stagnant and excess turbid phlegm displayed a purple tongue. Patients with a pattern of phlegm mixed with blood stasis manifested stasis macula on a purple tongue with sublingual varicosity. Regarding the tongue coating, patients with a pattern of exuberant liver fire and hyperactivity of yang due to yin deficiency manifested a yellow, thin tongue coating, and a white or yellow, greasy tongue coating was seen primarily in patients with a pattern of stagnant and excess turbid phlegm or a pattern of phlegm mixed with blood stasis. Hypertension is divided into three stages according to the associated clinical manifestations. In stage one, patterns of exuberant liver fire and hyperactivity of yang due to yin deficiency were the most common with a tongue that appeared red or crimson with a thin, yellow coating. The illness was not considered to be serious in the first stage. Patterns of stagnant and excess turbid phlegm were primarily seen in stage two disease with an enlarged, pale tongue and a greasy white or yellow tongue coating. A pattern of phlegm mixed with blood stasis dominated stage three with stasis macula on a purple tongue and a greasy white or yellow tongue coating. Clinically, using tongue diagnosis as the primary foundation for determining the stage of disease combined with other symptoms can insure that patients are given effective therapeutics according to the stage and type of disease, treating liver and kidney in first stage disease, resolving turbid phlegm in second stage disease, and treating phlegm and blood stasis simultaneously in third stage disease. Wang[8] observed the sublingual veins of 92 patients with hypertension and found that the age of the patient and course of disease were closely related to changes in the sublingual veins. Namely, that the older the patient, and the longer the disease had been present, the greater the widening, lengthening, curvature, distention, increase in collateral branches, and deeper the color of the sublingual vessels. Observation of changes in the sublingual vessels was valuable for syndrome differentiation within hypertension, and for judging the therapeutic effects of treatment and the prognosis for the disease.

Gong[9] studied 304 cases of hypertension focusing on the pathological appearance of the tongue appearance using fixed quantitative research methods and found that the nature of the tongue varied according to the syndrome. The tongue reflected the degree of excess or deficiency of the condition as well as the pattern of disease. Flaring up of liver fire with a prickly tongue was the most common pattern. A pattern of hyperactive yang due to hypoactive yin was associated with a feeble tongue shape that is known to appear primarily in syndromes of hyperactivity of liver yang. A fissured and enlarged tongue with teeth marks was seen primarily in syndromes of excess phlegm damp where the pathological mechanism was phlegm damp invading the enlarged tongue causing the fissures. All the changes seen in the tongues accorded with classifications within Chinese medicine pathology.

2. Coronary Heart Disease (CHD)

Coronary heart disease (CHD) is a severe disease that human beings encounter and by which they are frequently threatened. Sun[10] observed the dynamic appearance of the tongues of 366 patients who had CHD before and after treatment. The results shows that there were nine tongue colors that appeared including dark red, pale, pale and dark, light red, light purple, purple and dark, red, crimson and purple. Among them, dark red was the most common color comprising 37.70% of the tongues. In females, pale and pale dark tongues were the most common, and purple red or purple dark were the most common in males.

Jiao[11] conducted research on 150 patients with CHD and found that enlarged, light purple tongues with teeth marks and congestion of the sublingual veins was often was seen in patients who experienced angina pectoris with exertion, but that thin, light red tongues with normal sublingual veins were always present in individuals with variable angina pectoris.

3. Angina Pectoris

There are no obvious changes in the appearance of the tongue with moderate angina pectoris; however, the appearance of the tongue changes in cases of physiological or pathological obstruction. A pale, fat, tender tongue is usually associated with a differentiation of qi and yang deficiency. This is consistent with a decline in function of the left side of the heart while a blue and purple tongue is usually associated with CHD in which the dominant pattern is blood stasis. It is also consistent with the changes in blood circulation that occur in CHD patients. Changes in the sublingual vessels are closely related to CHD, Zhang[12] observed 100 patients with ischemic cardiovascular and cerebrovascular diseases and found that 100% of patients had dilated vessels in the internal and middle regions, 78.51% had them in the external region, 98.81% of patients had distorted internal and middle regions, 83.33% had a distorted external region, and in patients with spots, internal and middle regions averaged 92.85%.

4. Myocardial Infarction

Gao[13] used a tongue camera to observe special appearances of the tongue in 69 patients with acute myocardial infarction (AMI) and found a high percent of eroded spots on the front part of tongue, nearly 43.48% in early stage AMI. It had auxiliary significance for early diagnosis. The rule for changes in the tongue coating of AMI patients was thin to greasy and back to thin, and white to yellow then back to white. As the state of the disease became more serious, eroded coating or a tongue without coating emerged most frequently, and the rate of red tongues decreased while the rate of crimson and purple tongues increased. After thrombolytic treatment, Liang[14] observed changes in the progression of the tongue coating. He evaluated the syndrome, symptoms and tongues of 24 patients with AMI and found that the appearance of the tongue body changed from light red to red and the coating went from thin yellow to thick yellow. In the second week, white coating increased and yellow coating decreased with the stabilization of the illness. Regarding the thickness of the coating, thick coating appeared more frequently than thin coating, and the rate of thick yellow coating increased during the peak period of the disease.

Sun[15] determined the characteristics of and the rules that govern the changes in the tongue during the process of AMI. Generally, changes in coating that reflected an unfavorable prognosis were from thin to greasy, and yellow to black; changes were in the reverse direction in the case of a good prognosis. A white coating usually appeared in the early stages of disease suggesting that the disease was not serious and had few complications. A turn for the good was the case anytime a white fur appeared during the process. On the other hand, if a greasy yellow coating was continuously present or turned into a black coating, it suggested a serious disease with a bad prognosis. Therefore, appearance of the tongue reflected the degree of illness and indicated the prognosis.

5. Arrhythmia (Atrial Fibrillation)

Liu[16] treated 78 cases of premature heartbeat, differentiating the syndrome primarily by examining the appearance of the tongue, with *Píng Lù Tāng* (平律汤) which is composed of *dān shēn* (Radix et Rhizoma Salviae Miltiorrhizae, 丹参), *kǔ shēn* (Radix Sophorae Flavescentis, 苦参), *xuán shēn* (Radix Scrophulariae, 玄参), *yù jīn* (Radix Curcumae, 郁金), *jiǎo gǔ lán* (Rhizoma seu Herba Gynostemmatis Pentaphylli, 绞股蓝) as the basic formula. Modifications were made to treat six different syndromes. The syndrome of stagnant and excess phlegm heat with blockage of the heart vessels was usually seen in viral myocarditis, pulmonary heart diseases and the acute attack stage of hypertensive cardiopathy, and manifested as a red tongue with a greasy, yellow coating and stasis maculae on both sides of tongue. The treatment principle was to remove phlegm heat with a decoction of the formula *Huáng Lián Wēn Dǎn Tāng* (黄连温胆汤) modified. The syndrome of qi stagnation and blood stasis with failure of the chest yang to spread was usually seen in rheumatic heart failure, coronary heart disease and myocarditis, and manifested as a red or crimson tongue with stasis maculae. The syndrome of yin deficiency with exuberant fire and phlegm fire disturbing the heart was usually seen in the acute attack stage of myocarditis, pulmonary heart diseases and hypertensive cardiopathy, and manifested as a red, dry tongue with a greasy, yellow coating. The treatment principle was to nourish yin in order to quell the pathogenic fire, remove phlegm heat and calm the heart. The formula used was a decoction of *Huáng Lián Ē Jiāo Tāng* (黄连阿胶汤) combining with a decoction of *Wēn Dǎn Tāng* (温胆汤) modified. The syndrome of qi and blood deficiency with deficient heart yang was usually seen in rheumatic myocarditis, and manifested as an enlarged, light red tongue. The treatment principle was to benefit the qi and nourish the blood while warming the yang to replenish the kidney. The formula used was a decoction of *Guī Pí Tāng* (归脾汤) combined with a decoction of *Shēn Fù Tāng* (参附汤) modified. The syndrome of deficiency of both qi and yin with disturbance of the heart mind was usually seen in cases of vegetative nerve function disturbance and manifested as a dry, red tongue without coating. The premature heartbeat always happened during the resting state. The treatment principle was to benefit the qi and nourish the yin, and calm the heart. The formula used was a decoction of *Wǔ Shēn Tāng* (五参汤) or *Zhì Gān Cǎo Tāng* (炙甘草汤). The syndrome of deficiency of both heart and kidney yang and the syndrome of blood stasis blocking the channels were usually seen in rheumatic myocarditis and manifested as an enlarged, light purple tongue with teeth marks and a thin white coating. The treatment principle was to replenish the heart and warm the kidney, nourish blood and activate blood circulation to recover the pulse. The formula used was a decoction of *Shēn Fù Tāng* (参附汤) combined with a decoction of *Guì Zhī Gān Cǎo Long Gǔ Mǔ Lì Tāng* (桂枝甘草龙骨牡蛎汤) modified. The rate of efficacy was 91.0%.

Atrial fibrillation is one kind of arrhythmia, and it is divided into two types, paroxysmal and permanent. Ye[17] observed two kinds of changes in the appearance of the tongue, and characterized the nature of both types: the percentage of pale tongues in paroxysmal atrial fibrillation is greater while the percentage of purple, dark red, fat tongues in permanent atrial fibrillation is greater because the ejection function of the left cardiac ventricle decreases along with cardiac output. Most delayed type patients display a pattern of yang deficiency and blood stasis, so the tongue is purple and fat. The coating of patients with atrial fibrillation is a thin, white coating. If accompanied by heart failure, there is often a greasy coating which is explained by the pathogenesis of yang deficiency and water insulting. If the coating became greasier and thicker, the disease is becoming more serious due to the existence of other accompanying diseases.

6. Wind Stroke (Cerebral Hemorrhage)

Since the appearance of the tongue reflects the condition of the *zang-fu* organs, its appearance is significant in distinguishing the location of disease, the severity of the condition and the deficiency or excess of the syndrome as well as informing the treatment according to syndrome differentiation and estimating the prognosis for a disease. In the premonitory stage of stroke, the patient should undergo a special examination to look for the appearance of a stiff tongue with an unclear voice, numbness of the tongue, tongue pain or frequent protrusion of tongue in order to prevent a stroke. In the acute stage of stroke, clinical manifestations include a stiff tongue, stammering and a deviated tongue due to exuberant liver yang suddenly disturbing the brain channel caused by liver yin deficiency where the brain blood vessels are ischemic due to obstruction or bleeding after bursting. If there is a sudden attack of stroke, a protruding, licking, or shortened and contracted tongue are all serious signs, and measures to save the patient should be taken immediately. In the sequelae stage of a stroke, the tongue can manifest as trembling, flaccid or deviated due to a deficiency of both qi and blood, and liver wind stirring. In the end, a stroke is difficult to recover from, and the protruding tongue cannot be drawn back into the mouth easily due to numbness and

hypoesthesia of tongue. A deviated tongue indicates the recurrence of a stroke, and a shortened and contracted tongue suggests a critical condition[18].

Yang[19] observed 50 cases of cerebral hemorrhage and cerebral infarction which were all in the acute stage as diagnosed by a CT of the head and found that those with a cerebral hemorrhage primarily displayed a red tongue body with greasy yellow coating. An enlarged light red (or white) tongue with watery, thin, white coating was usually seen in cerebral infarction. This means the pathology of cerebral hemorrhage is liver yang rising suddenly and sharply due to deficiency of both the liver and kidney yin with the orifices confused by liver wind rising with phlegm. The therapeutic principle was to nourish yin in order to suppress hyperactive yang and to suppress hyperactive yang by calming endogenous wind, clearing heat and resolving phlegm. However, people who were constitutionally overweight, or who indulged in smoking and drinking were more likely to experience cerebral infarction where the pathology was blood vessels obstructed by turbid phlegm because of the retention of fluid due to qi and spleen deficiency. The treatment principle was to benefit qi, activate blood circulation and smooth the channels by tonifing the spleen to resolve phlegm. Based on comprehensive analysis of the data obtained through the four examinations and observation of the tongue, using treatment based on differentiation of syndromes significantly shortened the course of disease and enhanced the cure rate with a simultaneous decrease in the rate of disability.

Guo[20] treated 480 cases of wind stroke basing on the syndrome differentiation according to changes in the appearance of the tongue. For the syndrome of liver fire flaring upward, the appearance of the tongue was normal or deviated and red or dark red in color with a thin, yellow or a thick or even brown coating without fluid. The therapeutic principles employed were to remove liver fire and resuscitate by calming endogenous wind. The formula given was *Tiān Má Gōu Téng Yǐn* (天麻钩藤饮) modified. For the syndrome of stirring wind due to yin deficiency, the tongue was deviated or trembling and contracted with a red mirror-like tongue or a thin, yellow or white coating. The therapeutic principles employed were to nourish the liver and kidney and suppress the hyperactive liver to subdue yang. The formula used was *Zhèn Gān Xī Fēng Tāng* (镇肝熄风汤) modified. For the syndrome of stagnancy and retention of phlegm damp, the tongue was deviated and pale or dark red with a greasy, white or yellow, or even thick yellow coating. The treatment principles were to clear phlegm to smooth the channels and clear the mind for resuscitation. The formula was *Wēn Dǎn Tāng* (温胆汤) modified. For the syndrome of phlegm heat and blood stasis, the tongue was deviated, stiff and contracted while the color was red or dark red with stasis maculae with a thick greasy yellow, yellow brown or even black coating. The treatment principle was to removing blood stasis and clear heat, to employ catharsis to remove obstruction in the channels and eliminate phlegm for resuscitation. The formula was *Qīng Qì Huà Tán Wán* (清气化痰丸) modified. For the syndrome of blood stasis due to deficiency of qi, the tongue was deviated, flaccid, trembling, contracted and enlarged while the color was pale with stasis maculae and a thin white or greasy white coating. Benefiting qi and activating blood circulation to smooth the channels were the therapeutic principles and *Bǔ Yáng Huán Wǔ Tāng* (补阳还五汤) was the major formula that was modified. The rate of efficacy was 91%.

Fang[21] treated and diagnosed 675 cases of stroke basing on the appearance of the tongue with reference to CT scans of the head. He found that for ischemic apoplexy, the *zang-fu* organs type was mainly associated with a crimson or dark red tongue with a greasy yellow or dry yellow coating, and the channel type always manifested as a crimson and dark red or as a pale dark tongue with white greasy, thin yellow or greasy yellow coating. For hemorrhagic apoplexy, the channel type manifested as a red or pale dark tongue with white or yellow greasy coating and the *zang-fu* organs type was associated with a crimson or dark red tongue with yellow greasy or dry coating. Combining tongue diagnosis with CT scans allowed the researchers to diagnose and classify the disease objectively.

APPLICATION OF TONGUE DIAGNOSIS TO THE DIAGNOSIS AND TREATMENT OF LUNG DISEASES

Tongue diagnosis is significant in the diagnosis and treatment of chronic bronchitis, pulmonary heart disease and lung cancer.

1. SARS (Severe Acute Respiratory Syndrome)

SARS, also called infective atypical pneumonia, is strongly infective and transmits rapidly. Since November 2002, it has spread across many countries and areas, especially in our own country of China, and people still retain a lingering fear of it. In Chinese medicine, SARS belongs to "warm epidemics" (*wēn yì*, 温疫) which contains its own special theory and abundant experiments on treatment. Treating SARS by combining Chinese medicine with biomedicine can not only

reduce the dosage of hormones and toxic side effects, but can also improve pulmonary inflammatory lesions, effusion and fibrosis. It is also significant in preventing the patient's condition from worsening [22].

Liu[23] observed the appearance of the tongue in 193 cases of SARS combined with a questionnaire and found that in the early stage, usually one to five days after being infected, the tongue appeared pale or red with a thin white or thin yellow greasy coating. The middle stage occurs three to ten days after onset and is characterized by a dark red or purplish red tongue with a white or yellow greasy coating. The peak stage usually occurs within seven to fourteen days after the disease begins and manifests with a red or deep dark red tongue with white or yellow greasy coating. After ten to fourteen days, the recovery stage begins, and the tongue appears light red or tender with teeth marks and a slight or dry thin coating on it, or is pale or dark with a thin greasy coating. These results show a certain relationship between the patient's condition and the appearance of the tongue. It was therefore significant to study on the appearance of the tongue in order to analyze the condition and speculate on the prognosis.

Zhou[24] performed quantitative analysis on the appearance of the tongues of 224 patients and discussed how the appearance correlated with their condition. The pale dark or purple tongue with a thick yellow or white greasy coating indicates a serious situation where attention should be paid to strengthening and benefiting the qi and blood circulation, activating blood circulation and resolving dampness by tonifying the spleen and stomach. Pulmonary lesions were the principal pathology. Changes in the appearance of the tongue reflected the degree of severity of the pulmonary lesions. For instance, a purple dark tongue with a yellow or yellow greasy coating indicated that the locus of infection was present in two or more lobes of the lungs. If the tongue was pale with white coating, there were be fewer loci of infection.

2. Chronic Bronchitis and Pulmonary Heart Disease

Wu[25] found that changes in tongue quality and coating reflect the state of such conditions as chronic bronchitis and pulmonary heart disease, with or without a new infection, and with or without blood stasis. He found that that chronic bronchitis and pulmonary heart disease result in a pale tongue with a slippery thin white coating from deficiency of the spleen with failure to transport, water damp, and turbid phlegm reverse attacking; if the tongue is dark red and the coating changes to yellow from white, and there are fine particles that are difficult to scrape off, it is the result of spleen deficiency and prolonged phlegm damp transforming into heat, and phlegm heat damp saliva accumulation. If the tongue is red and corpulent, and there are small cracks on the tongue surface, the coating is white, broken and curd-like, there is little fluid and brightness, it is a syndrome of depletion of the spleen yang with coagulation and obstruction of damp cold and turbid phlegm obstructing the lung. This kind of appearance is often seen in critical condition pulmonary heart disease. If there is a yellow coating on the tongue surface of a pulmonary heart disease patient, it indicates that the patient suffers from pulmonary heart disease with a concurrent infection. It indicates blood stasis when the tongue is red with blue spots and ecchymosis on both sides of the tongue with a coating that looks exfoliated, or when the tongue is dark red with engorged blue vessels. Sun[26] divided pulmonary heart disease into four types on the basis of the appearance of the tongue: stagnation in the lung where the tongue is red with a yellow greasy coating; accumulation of phlegm damp in the lung where the tongue is red with a white greasy coating; deficiency of both lung and kidney where the tongue is crimson with a white greasy coating or peeling of the coating; deficiency of the lung, spleen and kidney where the tongue is dry and dark purple with a white greasy and white slippery coating. Liu[27] observed the tongue quality in 61 cases of pulmonary heart disease and found that in an acute attack of pulmonary heart disease, 41 patients had a predominantly red tongue amounting to 67.2%, and 32 patients had a predominantly greasy coating, amounting to 52.3%.

3. Lung Cancer

Clinical research showed that a tongue indicative of blood stasis usually accompanied lung cancer. Chen[28-29] explained this phenomenon by measuring the levels of TXB_2 and 6-keto-$PGF_{1\alpha}$, and this kind of appearance of the tongue was further associated with disorders of the blood platelets. Blood platelets can be synthesized into thrombin cord A_2 which promotes hemagglutination and is released to contract blood vessels thereby increasing the total viscosity of the blood. Therefore, the appearance of the tongue is created by the disturbance of microcirculation. The presence of a blood stasis tongue had no relation to the age of the patient. Regarding the appearance of the blood stasis tongue, varicosity of the sublingual veins tended to occur much more in patients with metastasis than in those without metastasis.

Su[30] observed and analyzed the tongues of 380 patients suffering from

primary lung cancer and found that the appearance of the tongue is valuable in dividing lung cancer into stages. If there is a red tongue with a thin moist coating, we can infer that the cancer is in an early stage. If there is a red or purple tongue with a thick curd-like coating, we can infer the cancer is in middle or late stage. 213 patients in this group had a purple tongue and amounted to 56.05%. It suggests improvement of a disease when a purple tongue changes to red, a dim tongue changes to bright, the coating changes from thick to thin, or from bare to thin. If the opposite occurs, the patient's condition is considered to be deteriorating. If the tongue is crimson red with little coating or without coating, it suggests the depletion of stomach qi, and the prognosis is unfavorable. Tongue diagnosis can reflect the tolerance patients have for radiation and can serve as a reference for determining the proper dosage of radiation. The appearance of the tongue can also serve as a guide for treatment and the use of pharmaceutical drugs.

4. Chronic Obstructive Pulmonary Disease (COPD)

COPD is a kind of chronic respiratory disease in which the flow of air is obstructed due to chronic bronchitis and emphysema. The course of the disease is progressive, and it may be combined with bronchial hypersensitivity. This disease can cover cough due to internal injury, asthmatic syndromes and lung swelling syndromes in Chinese medicine, and is closed related to the syndrome of phlegm leading to blood stasis which involves a simultaneous disorder of the qi and blood. Just as *Dan-xi's Methods* (*Dān Xī Xīn Fǎ*, 丹溪心法) says, "*cough due to lung swelling which manifests as tossing about in bed is caused by the obstruction of qi circulation due to phlegm with blood stasis*". Gong[31] treated 80 patients who were in the acute aggravative stage of COPD displaying a dark red tongue with a yellow greasy coating. They were treated by inhaling an aerosolized version of *Yán Chuǎn Píng Hé Jì* (炎喘平合剂) which is composed of *huáng qín* (Radix Scutellariae, 黄芩), *fǎ bàn xià* (Rhizoma Pinelliae Praeparatum, 法半夏), *jié gěng* (Radix Platycodonis, 桔梗), *yuǎn zhì* (Radix Polygalae, 远志). After inhalation, coughing and gasping of the patients improved as phlegm heat was cleared through the smooth expectoration of sputum that decreased in volume. Regarding the appearance of the tongues, dark red tongues with a yellow greasy coating vanished gradually after treatment. Tang[32] observed the tongues of 368 patients who were experiencing an acute attack of COPD and found that the existence of a blood stasis tongue was related to the severity of the patient's condition and usually indicated a serious condition with subsequent infection, an asthma attack or worsening of asthma, or even accompanying pulmonary heart disease. Blood gas analysis 24 hours after hospitalization showed that an increase in $PaCO_2$ and a decrease in SaO_2 were important factors in the appearance of a blood stasis tongue in COPD.

APPLICATION OF TONGUE DIAGNOSIS TO THE DIAGNOSIS AND TREATMENT OF SPLEEN AND STOMACH DISEASES

"The tongue is the outward manifestation of the spleen and stomach, the coating is the stomach qi that has been steamed upward." Changes in the appearance of the tongue have are closely related to spleen and stomach disease. Responses in the appearance of the tongue diseases of the spleen and stomach are quick and accurate. Tongue diagnosis can be used to make judgements about diseases of the spleen and stomach.

1. Chronic Gastritis

The existence of Helicobacter pylori is closely related to the tongue coating. Recently, scholars within China and from abroad have begun to consider chronic gastritis to be related to infection by H. pylori. Wei[33] observed that the tongue coating of gastritis patients infected with H. pylori was a white greasy coating, a yellow greasy coating or a yellow coating. When H. pylori invades the gastric mucosa, the spleen yang is encumbered by damp and the coating is primarily white and greasy. If the infection by H. pylori is not completely eradicated, it will transform into heat and a yellow greasy coating or a yellow coating will appear. Infection by H. pylori does not affect the quality of the tongue.

Wang[34] cleared heat toxin to treat patients with erosive gastritis diagnosed by endoscopy. Wang observed clinical symptoms, gastro scopic findings, pathological findings, the presence of H. pylori and tongue coating before and after treatment. The results showed that the degree of erosion of the stomach lining, whether infected by H. pylori or not, and the degree of severity of the symptoms were closely related to the tongue coating. Yellow coating appeared frequently in people with severe symptoms and erosion, or in those infected by H. pylori. However, the rate appearance of yellow coating after treatment (27.2%) was much less than before treatment (82.19%) (P<0.01). Huang[35] diagnosed 120 patients with chronic superficial gastritis via gastroscopy and pathological

examination, and researched the relationship between the appearance of the tongue and infection by H. pylori. Huang found that 43.3% of the patients had detectable levels of H. pylori. The types of tongue coatings observed in descending order of frequency were as follows: yellow greasy coating, white greasy coating, thin yellow coating and thin white coating. As for the tongue body, the appearance in descending order of frequency was as follows: dark purple tongue, red tongue, pale tongue and light red tongue. In conclusion, changes in the appearance of the tongue in patients with chronic superficial gastritis had a certain relationship with infection by H. pylori.

Xie[36] observed the relationship between images of the gastric mucosa and the appearance of the tongue in different types of chronic gastritis and found that patients with congestive and exudative gastritis had a normal thin white coating. Regarding the erosive type, flat and bulging types were both associated with a white greasy coating. Eroded coating was due to deficiency of both qi and yin, and usually appeared in the atrophic type while a thick yellow coating appeared with the reflux type. For the type with hyperplasia of the rugae, erosion of the coating could be due to vital deficiency or a greasy coating could be due to excess turbid evil. Therefore, if the patient's condition was not serious, the coating manifested as a thin white coating and the gastroscopic image was of a congestive or exudative type. If the patient's condition was severe, the coating manifested as a thick greasy coating with gastroscopic images of the erosive and reflux types of gastritis. For the patient with deficiency of the normal qi, eroded coating and a gastroscopic image of the atrophic or hemorrhagic type of gastritis was usually seen.

Tongue quality and coating corresponds to the extent of the disease in gastritis. He[37] found that most tongue coatings associated with chronic superficial gastritis patients were yellow or thick, and most tongue coatings associated with chronic atrophic gastritis were yellow thick coatings. Inflammation faded gradually with treatment. He proposed that the formation of a yellow coating probably had something to do with gastric inflammation. Cheng[38] found that the course of disease for superficial gastritis is short. There is a high percentage of red tongues associated with superficial gastritis than atrophic gastritis or atrophic gastritis accompanied by epithelial metaplasis; however, the percentage of blue tongues associated with the latter, considered a precancerous lesion, is higher. Ding[39] found that in chronic atrophic gastritis, 60% of cases corresponded to deficiency of stomach yin type where the tongue is red with little fluid and no coating, so

caution should be used when employing drugs whose nature is pungent, dry and hot.

2. Gastric and Duodenal Ulcers

He[37] found that in the active stage of an ulcer, most tongues had a yellow coating or a thick coating. The coating normalized when the ulcer was cured. A thick yellow coating would be present when an ulcer was accompanied by chronic superficial gastritis. The tongue often exhibited no changes in the presence of a duodenal ucler; obvious changes were only evident if it was accompanied by superficial gastritis or a gastric ulcer. Therefore, changes in the tongue offer a certain value in making judgments regarding the gastric diseases mentioned above. When the coating changed from thick to thin, or from yellow to white, there was a tendency toward improvement, and a tendency towards a worsening of the condition if the changes were in the opposite direction. But patients with a similar degree of pathological change may have significantly different tongues. Especially in males and females, the unique tendency of the tongue of an individual has great reference value, and the relative changes in the appearance of the tongue can be of help in judging whether there is a perforation or not. It can also be of assistance in diagnosing the location and nature of the perforation.

Zhu[40] found that the tongue displayed different features during the active, healing and scar stages of a duodenal bulbar ulcer. A normal light red tongue with thin white coating was characteristic of the scar stage. During the healing stage, half of the tongues were of normal color and half of abnormal color with a think yellow coating. During the active stage, the color of tongue was pale, red or dark red with a thick yellow greasy or thick white greasy coating. An abnormal tongue body usually appeared in the active stage and sometimes appeared in the healing stage.

Zhu[41] observed the tongues of patients with upper digestive track disease and found that superficial gastritis manifested as a light red tongue with a thin white coating, and atrophic gastritis manifested as a dark tongue with a greasy coating. Comparing these two types, the first is less serious because of the normal appearance of the tongue, and the second is indicative of a more serious condition because of the abnormal appearance of the tongue caused by blood stagnating in the stomach channels with obstruction of the middle *jiao* by turbid dampness due to deficiency of the spleen and stomach. Regarding peptic ulcers, a pale tongue with white coating was seen primarily in duodenal bulbar ulcers, and a red tongue with yellow coating was seen usually in complex ulcers. Duodenal bulbar ulcers

therefore mainly belonged to the syndrome of deficient cold of the spleen and stomach whereas gastric and complex ulcers mainly fell within the syndrome of qi stagnation with heat in the stomach although the peptic gastric ulcer was attributed to the stomach. In the case of tumors of the upper digestive tract, the typical tongue appeared dark with a yellow greasy or black coating for which the pathology was accumulated noxious damp and heat.

Wang[42] found that the crimson area on the tip of the tongue will tend to increase with an existing gastric perforation, and decrease with an existing duodenal perforation. The tongue color of most patients with a simple gastric or duodenal perforation was light red, red or crimson; however, most tongues were blue, purple or pale with the existence of a cancerous perforation or hemorrhage of the digestive tract. If the tongue was light red, the width of the perforation was less than 0.5 cm, and the peritoneal effusion was less than 300 ml. If the tongue was red, crimson or purple, the perforation was bigger than 0.5 cm, and the peritoneal effusion was more than 300 ml. A white coating suggested mild obstruction with an existing gastric or duodenal perforation. However, a yellow or black coating suggested a more severe condition.

3. Gastroesophageal Reflux Disease(GERD)

Ding[43] found that the patients with GERD experienced changes in the color of the tongue that included pale, red, crimson and purple which corresponded to changes in the gastric mucosa that included a pale appearance with edema, congestion, erythema and erosion. The relationship between the tongue coating and the rate of H. pylori infection was clear. A yellow greasy mirror-like tongue coating appeared more frequently than a white greasy coating, more coating occurred more frequently than little or no coating, and yellow thin coating occurred more frequently than thin white coating. The conclusion was therefore that changes in the appearance of the tongue were related to both gastroscopic images of GERD and the rate of H. pylori infection. Moreover, changes in the tongue color were related to changes in the color of the gastric mucosa, and changes in the tongue coating reflected the degree of H. pylori infection. Yang[44] observed the tongues of patients with reflux gastritis and found that the relationship with changes in the gastric mucosa was unclear, but that the relationship with observations via gastroscope were obvious. That is to say, a crimson or dark red tongue with a yellow greasy coating appeared in the bile

reflux type, and a light red tongue with white greasy coating appeared in the intestinal fluid reflux type.

4. Gastric Carcinoma

Lin[45] found the appearance of the tongue in patients with precancerous lesions and chronic atrophic gastritis was dark red or bluish purple with stasis maculae and a greasy coating, or with teeth marks and fissures, or even sublingual varicose veins or stasis spots. Observation of the microcirculation on the tip of the tongue showed that enlarged malformed capillary loops expanded with static blood. The seepage of dark red blood was obvious and the blood renology abnormal. A smear of the tongue coating showed that lingual epithelial cells were hyperkeratotic with an increased count against the dirty background of the smear which was full of white cells. The pH value was higher and the CEA obviously increased in the saliva. The characteristic changes were therefore significant in enhancing the detection of CAG and also for providing an objective basis for clinical syndrome differentiation, treatment, and determining the effect of treatment.

5. Acute Appendicitis

Yang[46] found that the appearance of the tongue in patients with acute appendicitis adhered to a certain rule. When there was a perforation, a suppuration or gangrene of the appendix perforation or suppuration, most tongue coatings were white and slippery or yellow and greasy. Most patients with simple appendicitis had a thin white coating. Statistical analysis showed that the diagnosis based on the appearance of the tongue accorded with preoperation and postoperation at a rate of 93.5%. Wang[47] found that different pathologic types of acute appendicitis followed different rules in terms of how the tongue changed. That is to say, on the basis of a white or thin yellow coating on the tongue tip, the quality of the tongue will become red or crimson with suppurating appendicitis, and a thick greasy coating will appear. Not only will the tongue tip, color and coating change, but ecchymosis or spots will occur when there is gangrene. The red region of the tongue will enlarge when appendicitis is accompanied by peritonitis. In severe cases, it may even look bright like a light. If peritonitis is prolonged and not cured, the white greasy or yellow greasy coating will peel. When there is an imbalance between water and eletrolytes, except for when the original color deepens, the surface of the tongue will often become cracked or dry, and there will be a brown yellow or brown black coating in the middle of the tongue.

APPLICATION OF TONGUE DIAGNOSIS TO THE DIAGNOSIS AND TREATMENT OF LIVER AND GALLBLADDER DISEASES

Recent research has found that the tongue has a certain relationship with infection by the hepatitis B virus, and on the basis of its character, we can make judgements about diseases that involve infections of the liver and gallbladder, guide treatment and evaluate the prognosis. Changes in the quality of the tongue and the coating can reflect the tendency and condition of different phases of a disease.

1. Hepatitis B and Liver Cancer

Yuan[48] analyzed the appearance of the tongue and the liver function of 200 patients with the hepatitis virus and found that the closest relationships were between the disturbance of protein metabolism as reflected mainly in changes in tongue quality, and increases of ALT and bilirubin as primarily reflected in changes in the tongue coating. For example, a person with hypoproteinemia usually had a pale tongue with teeth marks on the sides of the tongue, but occasionally had a red tender tongue. If the hypoproteinemia increased along with the level of bilirubin, the coating was yellow and greasy. In hyperproteinemia, the tongue primarily manifested as red and tender with a yellow greasy coating. Also, dark red tongues with stasis maculae were seen in some patients with chronic active hepatitis. For cases where the level of ALT increased, the appearance of the tongue primarily manifested as red with a yellow greasy coating though a portion of the tongues appeared normal. For cases where the level of bilirubin increased, most patients had a red tongue with a yellow greasy coating while there was a small minority of patients with a white greasy coating. Regarding hepatitis with jaundice, the tongue quality was primarily purple with stasis. Observing the appearance of the tongue is not only useful for evaluating changes in the liver function of patients, and for speculating upon the prognosis and the direction of disease, but is also good for enhancing the effects of the treatment of viral hepatitis by Chinese medicine combined with biomedicine.

Zhang[49] observed the tongue and pathology of patients with chronic hepatitis B and found that there were no obvious changes in the tongue quality of those with chronic persistent hepatitis (CPH). The tongue was light red. There was fibroblastic proliferation, and the liver cells were loose and bright. In chronic active hepatitis (CAH), most tongues were red, dark purple or had signs of ecchymosis. When the tongue was red, there was mainly fragmented necrosis, borderline necrosis and focal necrosis. Changes in the tongue coating of those with chronic hepatitis had no obvious significance. The above results were basically the same as those of Luo. Luo[50] found that most of the tongues of patients with CAH are dark purple or display ecchymosis which suggests blood stasis obstructing the collaterals. The therapy should therefore be to nourish yin and disperse liver qi, and to add medicinals that activate blood circulation and remove blood stasis. The tongues of patients with CPH were mostly light red, so the therapy should be to clear the heat and toxins. Xia[51] found that the appearance of the tongue in asymptomatic carriers of the virus was normal which suggests only mild evils. If the tongue is a continuous dark purple or displays signs of eccchymosis, it suggests that the virus is replicating and is active. Medicinals whose nature is to activate blood and remove blood stasis should be added in order to prevent the cirrhosis of the liver. Zhao[52] proposed that drug use, dosage, time of drug use and regulation of drugs should be decided on the basis of tongue diagnosis. If the tongues of hepatitis B patients are pale and fat with a white greasy coating, it indicates a deficient spleen encumbered by damp, and medicinals to strengthen the spleen and resolve damp should be used. If the tongue and coating become normal, the dosage of medicinals that resolve damp should be reduced lest they injure the yin. At this point, high doses of medicinals used to strengthen the body's resistance and clear toxins should be used. Li[53] found that dark red tongues with a fat tongue body or teeth marks on both sides are often seen in the early stages of cirrhosis of the liver. In the compensatory phase, bluish purple tongues and bluish purple ecchymosis are often seen in clinic. In the decompensatory phase with less ascites, light red tongues and white greasy coatings are often seen. In the late stages of cirrhosis of the liver, there are reddish purple tongues with ecchymosis or spots and engorged sublingual vessels with a thin yellow greasy coating.

Li[54] speculated on the prognosis of patients with chronic hepatitis B by observing the appearance of their tongues and found that red tongues with teeth marks or with no tongue coating would fare badly. For those diagnosed with chronic active hepatitis, the disease would develop into cirrhosis of the liver, chronic severe hepatitis or even result in death if a red tongue with teeth marks and no coating appeared. If the tongue was pale or light red with coating and without teeth marks, the patient's condition would be relatively stable. Chronic

persistent hepatitis easily turned into chronic active hepatitis and developed into cirrhosis if the tongue was red with no coating. If the opposite was the case, the patient would improve.

He[55] found that chronic hepatitis B usually manifested as an excess syndrome with a red tongue with greasy coating and lots of saliva, or a dark tongue with stasis maculae or sublingual varicose veins. For these kinds of cases, herbs whose function is to activate blood circulation should be used to remove the blood stasis in order to prevent the development of hepatic fibrosis or even hepatic cirrhosis.

2. Cirrhosis of the Liver

Sun[56] verified that the appearance of the tongue of patients with hepatic cirrhosis was obviously different from that of a normal person, and manifested as purplish green, dark red and crimson with a white or yellow greasy coating, or even a peeled coating. Li[57] evaluated the severity of the patient's condition by examining the color of the tongue and changes in the tongue coating that included thickness or thinness, moistness or dryness, curdiness or greasiness, and treated the disease according to syndrome differentiation combining with the four examinations. In the type with accumulations and masses and the syndrome of spleen deficiency due to liver qi stagnation which was seen in the early stages of cirrhosis of the liver, the tongue was usually dark red or pale, or it had teeth marks. The treatment principle was to soothe the liver qi and tonify the spleen with the formula *Chái Hú Shū Gān Sǎn* (柴胡疏肝散) and *Sì Jūn Zǐ Tāng* (四君子汤) modified. The syndrome of qi stagnation and blood stasis which was seen in the compensatory phase of hepatic cirrhosis and the decompensatory phase of liver function impairment manifested as a purplish blue tongue with stasis maculae and spots. It was treated by soothing the liver qi to activate blood stasis and resolve masses with *Huó Xuè Huà Yū Tāng* (活血化瘀汤). The type with distention of the abdomen and the syndrome of stagnation of fluid damp was seen in the decompensatory stage of mild ascites and always manifested as a light red tongue with a white greasy or a thin white coating. It was treated by tonifying the spleen and resolving dampness with the formulas *Wǔ Líng Tāng* (五苓汤) and *Shí Pí Yǐn* (实脾饮). The syndrome of collaterals blocked by blood stasis was seen in the late stages of hepatic cirrhosis which manifested as a purplish red tongue with stasis maculae and sublingual varicose veins accompanied by the appearance of a thin yellow greasy coating. The treatment principle was to promote blood circulation to remove blood stasis and encourage diuresis with the formula *Gé Xià Zhú Yū Tāng* (膈下逐瘀汤).

3. Primary Hepatocarcinoma

Tong[58] found that a distinguishing purple or blue color on the left or right side of the tongue with stripes or irregularly shaped stasis maculae always appeared in patients with primary hepatocarcinoma. Occasionally, it presented on both sides of the tongue simultaneously. Tong named it the "liver *ying* line (*gān yǐng xiàn*, 肝瘿线)" whose pathology should be studied and discussed further. It was verified that the liver *ying* line is one of simple signs that can be employed in determining whether a patient is suffering from liver disease or not, and it had auxiliary significance in the diagnosis of middle or late stage primary hepatocarcinoma. Huang[59] found that the tongue quality was usually normal in stage Ⅰ and Ⅱ a hepatocarcinoma, and that a red or purple tongue with stasis maculae was seen mainly in stage Ⅱ b and Ⅲ. They therefore thought the tongue quality could reflect the degree of liver function as well as whether the hepatocarcinoma had metastasized or not. Wang[60] observed the appearance of the tongues of patients who had hepatocarcinoma with bleeding, and found that the color was primarily crimson or purplish green with a coating that was thick, dry and gray or black. For the patients without bleeding, a pale or light red tongue with a thick yellow coating appeared frequently. Changes in the appearance of the tongue during the course of treatment also possessed some distinctive features like the color of tongue body turning from light to deep (from light red to crimson or even green or purple), similar changes in the coating of the tongue (from thin white to thick yellow, gray or even black), and an increase in the coating of the tongue from thin to thick with dryness. The above manifestations indicated a progressive course of disease which was inclined toward bleeding and severe pathological lesions from blood stasis, toxins and deficiency of the body. In order to prevent hematorrhea, it was best to take medicines in advance whose functions were to clear heat and remove toxins, cool blood and stop bleeding, activate blood circulation and resolve blood stasis, and regulate the flow of qi and tonify the spleen. Also, medicines which can lead extra blood back to the vessels should be used to prolong the patient's life.

4. Cholecystitis and Cholelithiasis

LI[53] observed 69 patients with acute cholecystitis and found that most of their tongue coatings were yellow and greasy while some were white and greasy. Most of the tongues were red, especially on both the margins and the tip which suggested acute cholecystitis resulting from stagnation of liver and gallbladder

qi, and damp heat accumulation in the middle *jiao*. Ling[61] has reported that a thin white coating suggests chronic cholecystitis, that a crimson or red tongue with a deep color at the margins suggests acute cholecystitis, that cracks indicate recurrent inflammation, and that spots or ecchymosis indicate gallstones and severe inflammation.

APPLICATION OF TONGUE DIAGNOSIS TO THE DIAGNOSIS AND TREATMENT OF KIDNEY DISEASES

In diseases of the kidney, attention should be paid to tongue color, the tenderness or toughness of the tongue, teeth marks and the color beneath, and changes in the thickness or thinness of the coating. Du[62] also proposed that the observation of transverse line of tongue margin should be pay attention to. In his research for 32 cases of renal failure, 19 cases of the 23 moderate and severe patients have shown the vague or vanished transverse line of tongue margin, the accordant rate attained 82.6%. Reddish tongues suggest ample qi and blood. The incidence of pale tongues increases with a decline in kidney function, and this kind of tongue also has a certain relationship with edema and anemia. A pale tongue may occur with severe anemia, but sometimes the color of the tongue will not change even if there is a low hematocrit. On the other hand, a pale tongue may occur even if the hematocrit is not low and the biochemical conditions in the kidney are normal. This suggests doctors should remain alert and pay attention when there is a pale tongue in the presence of a kidney disease, especially in the event of kidney failure.

The pathological appearance of the tongue in chronic renal failure (CRF) includes a fat tongue body[63] and teeth marks. The fat tongue body results from low hemoglobin and blood viscosity while the formation of teeth marks result from the compression of the fat tongue body by the gums. Some patients display varying degrees of blood stasis which manifests as a tongue that is pale purple, dark red, dark purple, or has ecchymosis and is mainly due to yang deficiency of both the spleen and kidney which fail to transport blood leading to obstruction of the blood and vessels. Measurements of the conduction of tongue fluid in patients with CRF are obviously lower than in healthy people which suggests that pathological changes in CRF have a certain relationship to the tongue fluid. One manifestation of acute nephritis and nephrotic syndrome is a red tongue, but in this phase its nature is one of prosperity of normal qi, and evil qi does not matter. The tongues of CRF patients mainly have a thin white coating or a thin white greasy coating, especially in yang deficiency of both the spleen and kidney. The diagnostic value of tongue color in kidney diseases has not been verified, and is in need of further observation. The theory that a yellow coating suggests a heat syndrome and a white coating suggests a cold syndrome does not seem to be applicable in kidney diseases because yellow and white coatings often transform into each other during the development of kidney diseases. Transverse cracks at the margins of the tongue become shallower, flatter and more vague or disappear altogether often suggesting that kidney function is poor.

Wang[64] used cytochemistry and image pattern analysis to determine the chemical composition of the lingual epithelial cells of 272 patients with chronic renal failure who manifested four different syndromes including qi deficiency of the spleen and kidney, yin deficiency of the liver and kidney, yang deficiency of the spleen and kidney and deficiency of both yin and yang. The results showed quite different appearances of the tongue within the four syndromes. Within the syndrome of qi deficiency of the spleen and kidney, a pale tongue with a thin white coating comprised 58.8% of the patients, and an enlarged pale or dark tongue with a white watery greasy coating comprised 38.2%. Within the syndrome of yang deficiency of the spleen and kidney, an enlarged pale or dark tongue was the major feature and comprised 79.4% of the patients. A red tongue with little coating comprised 55.6% of patients with yin deficiency of the liver and kidney. Moreover, a red tongue was often seen together with a thin yellow or a thin greasy coating. Within the syndrome of deficiency of both yin and yang, there were no special features that manifested on the tongue which appeared as a pale or red tongue with yellow or little coating. The normal group had a light red tongue with a thin white moist coating 85% of the time.

APPLICATION OF TONGUE DIAGNOSIS IN THE DIAGNOSIS AND TREATMENT OF ENDOCRINE DISORDERS

Recently, more than ten years of research[65] suggests that there is a relationship between the tongue and endocrinopathy, that the appearance of the tongue not

only has something to do with factors relevant to the local tongue area, but that it can reflect conditions in the endocrine system. Plenty of endocrinopathies show up as specific changes on the tongue. The formation of a pale tongue is closely related to adrenocortical insufficiency; however, a bare red tongue has a certain relationship with hyperparathyroidism.

Tongue diagnosis is significant in the differentiation and treatment of diabetes[66-67]. Diabetes leads to severe pathological changes in the qi, blood and body fluids because diabetes involves a long course of disease with severe injury to the *zang-fu* organs resulting from yin deficiency and dry heat. The appearance of the tongue can promptly reflect pathological changes in diabetes, and offers a basis for therapeutic principles and treatment. For example, doctors should clear heat and nourish yin, promote the production of body fluids and quench thirst if a red, brightly colored tongue that might even have prickles on the tip with a dry thin coating is seen; if a dark red tongue with little fluid with little or no coating is seen, the principle of nourishing the liver and kidney, moistening dryness and quenching thirst should adopted; if a tender tongue with teeth mark on both sides of the tongue is seen, the spleen should be strengthened and doctors should replenish qi and promote the production of body fluids. Zhou[67] found in clinical observation that diabetes patients with a dark purple tongue with curved sublingual vessels had blood stasis, and that the extent of the blood stasis was related to the patient's condition and the onset of symtoms. It is important to pay attention to this in treatment, and medicinals that move blood and transform stasis should be used.

REFERENCES

1. Shao Hua, et al. Discussion of Therapeutic Methods and Comprehensive Pathological Changes in Warm Disease in Chinese Medicine. Chinese Journal of Modern Chinese Medicine, 2005, 1(2): 131-133

2. Du Song-song. Brief Discussion of Tongue Diagnosis in Warm Disease. Hubei Journal of Traditional Chinese Medicine, 1992, 14(5): 30-31

3. Song Wen-hai, et al. Discussion and Analysis of Ye Tian-shi and Tongue Diagnosis. Journal of the Jiangxi Academy of Chinese Medicine, 1993, 5 (1): 21-22

4. Liu Ji-zhi. Clinical Experience in Tongue Differentiation in Warm Damp. Journal of Practical Traditional Chinese Medicine, 1993, (1): 29-30

5. Zhang Bi-li. Discussion of the Syndrome and Treatment of the Crimson Tongue by Ye Tian-Shi. Tianjin Journal of Traditional Chinese Medicine, 1996, (2): 6-7

6. Huang Su-fang, et al. The Application of Tongue Diagnosis in the Purging and Expelling of Heat. Journal of Chinese Medicine, 1999, 34 (12): 43-44

7. Yang She-xiang. Analysis of Common Appearances of the Tongue in Hypertension. Journal of Henan Chinese Medicine, 1997, 12 (6): 45-47

8. Wang Fa-wei, et al. Controlled Observation of Sublingual Veins of Hypertensive Patients. Chinese Journal of Arteriosclerosis, 2004, 12 (4): 455-457

9. Gong Yi-ping, et al. Quantitative Research on Common Pathological Appearances of the Tongue and Analysis of the Correlation to Hypertension and its Syndromes. Chinese Journal of Traditional Chinese Medicine, 2005, 20 (12): 730-731

10. Jiao Qi-chao. Changes in the Appearance of the Tongue and the Significance in Patients with Coronary Heart Disease. Cardio and Cerebrovascular Journal of the Integration of Traditional Chinese and Western Medicine, 2003, 1 (1): 62

11. Sun Min, et al. Research on Tongue Diagnosis in Coronary Heart Disease. Journal of Information on Chinese Medicine, 2004, 21 (3): 51-53

12. Zhang Hua-yi, Predicting Coronary Heart Disease and Windstroke in the "Tongue Vessels". Journal of Practical TCM and Western Medicine, 1993, 6 (6): 389

13. Gao Xiu-mei. Special Appearances of the Tongue in Acute Myocardial Infarction. Journal of TCM, 1994, 35(3): 365

14. Liang Rong, et al. Research into the Law of and Changes in the Appearance of the Tongue in Patients with Acute Myocardial Infarction. Journal of Chinese Medicine, 2005, 33 (4): 61-63

15. Sun Yi-chun. Analysis of the Laws of and Changes in the Appearance of the Tongue in Patients with Acute Myocardial Infarction. Journal of the Liaoning College of Traditional Chinese Medicine, 2003, 5 (2): 107

16. Liu Di-gui, et al. Clinical Research on 78 Patients with Premature Heart Beat with Syndrome Differentiation via Inspection of the Tongue and Pulse. Chinese Journal of Modern Integration of Traditional Chinese and Western Medicine, 2005, 3 (5) : 428-429

17. Ye Yang-guang. Tongue Observation in 88 Cases of Chronic Atrial Fibrillation in the Elderly. Fujian Journal of TCM, 1992, 23 (2): 31-32

18. Yuan Jin-long. Discussion of an Introduction to Syndrome Differentiation According to Changes in the Appearance of the Tongue in Patients with Wind Stroke. Journal of Gansu Chinese Medicine, 2001, 14(5): 1-2

19. Yang Man-ju. Observation of the Appearance of the Tongue in 50 Cases of Acute Stage Cerebrovascular Disease. Chinese Journal of the Practical Integration of Traditional Chinese and Western Medicine. 2003, 3 (16): 12

20. Guo Yan, et al. The Relationship between the Appearance of the Tongue and Wind Stroke. Journal of Beijing Chinese Medicine, 2000, 3: 11-12

21. Fang Zhi-yong, et al. The Significance of Combining Tongue Diagnosis with CT Indications to Diagnose Acute Wind Stroke. Cardio-cerebral vascular Journal of the Integration of Traditional Chinese and Western Medicine, 2002, 2 (10): 577-578

22. Liu Yu-lan. Preventing SARS with the Integration of Chinese Medicine and Biomedicine. Chinese Journal of the Integration of Traditional Chinese and Western Medicine, 2003, 23 (7): 484-485

23. Liu Bao-yan, et al. Analysis of the Appearance of the Tongue in 193 patients with SARS. Journal of Research and Clinic in Chinese Medicine, 2003, 13 (7): 20-23

24. Zou Jin-pan, et al. Study of the Correlation in Quantitive Research between the Appearance of the Tongue and the Condition of Patients in 224 Cases of SARS. Chinese Journal of the Integration of Traditional Chinese and Western Medicine, 2003, 23 (10): 740-743

25. Wu Ji-chuan. Simple Discussion of the Application of Tongue Diagnosis to the Treatment of Chronic Bronchitis and Pulmonary Heart Disease. Hubei Journal of TCM, 2000,22 (12): 19

26. Sun Jie-min. Types and Prognosis of Changes in the Tongue in Pulmonary Heart Disease.

Current Journal of TCM and Western Medicine, 2000, 28 (1): 38

27. Liu Jian-wen, Tongue Observation in 61 Patients with Pulmonary Heart Disease. Tianjin Journal of Traditional Chinese Medicine, 1992, (2): 38-44

28. Chen Qun, et al. A Study of the Correlation between the Appearance of a Blood Stasis Tongue and TXA_2 / PGI_2 in the Plasma of Patients with Lung Cancer. Chinese Journal of the Integration of Traditional Chinese and Western Medicine, 2006, 26 (1): 71

29. Chen Qun, et al. Clinical Study of the Appearance of a Blood Stasis Tongue in 79 Patients with lung Cancer. Forum of Traditional Chinese Medicine, 2005, 20 (3):10-11

30. Su Jin-mei. Tongue Analysis in 380 Cases of Primary lung Cancer. Shanxi Journal of TCM, 2000, 16 (5):12-13

31. Gong Ju-mei, et al. Influence of the Atomized Inhalation of the Mixture Yan Chuan Ping on the Appearance of the Tongue in Patients in the Acute Exacerbation Stage of Chronic Obstructive Pulmonary Disease. Research on Nursing Science, 2001, 15 (3): 169

32. Tang Yong-xiang, et al. Study of the Appearance of a Blood Stasis Tongue in the Acute Exacerbation Stage of Chronic Obstructive Pulmonary Disease. Journal of Guangxi Chinese Medicine, 2004, 27 (2): 8-9

33. Wei Xue-qin, et al. Analysis of the Relationship between H. pylori and the Tongue and Coating of Patients with Chronic Gastritis. Sichuan Journal of TCM, 1999, 17 (11): 7-8

34. Wang Chang-hong, et al. Study in Changes in the Tongue Coating Before and After Treatment in 146 Patients with Erosive Gastritis. Journal of Chinese Medicine, 2003, 21 (8): 1272-1273

35. Huang Ming-han, et al. Clinical Observation in 120 Patients with Chronic Superficial Gastritis and Infection by H. pylori. Journal of the Liaoning College of Traditional Chinese Medicine, 2005, 7 (2): 99-100

36. Xie Jing, et al. Clinical Observation of the Relationship between the Tongue Coating and Endoscopic Classification of Gastritis. China Journal of Basic Medicine in Traditional Chinese Medicine, 2004, 10 (11): 50-51

37. He Jin-sen, et al. Tongue Observation in Patients with Peptic Ulcer and Chronic Gastritis. Tianjin Journal of Traditional Chinese Medicine, 2000, 17 (15): 16-17

38. Cheng Feng-qiao. Relevant Observations via Gastroscope and pathology of the Tongues of 900 Patients with Chronic Gastritis. Hebei Journal of TCM, 1999, 21 (11): 349-350

39. Ding Chuang-ye. Simple Analysis of the Tongues of Patients with Chronic Gastritis. Journal of Practical TCM and Western Medicine, 1996, 9 (2): 111

40. Zhu Guo-shu, et al. The Significance and Characteristics of the Appearance of the

Tongue in Stage Ⅲ Duodenobulbar Ulcer. Journal of the Fujian College of Traditional Chinese Medicine, 2003, 13 (5): 10-11

41. Zhu Cui-zu. Analysis of the Appearance of the Tongue in 600 Patients with Diseases of the Upper Digestive Tract. Clinical Journal of Anhui Traditional Chinese Medicine, 2000, 12 (6): 518-519

42. Wang Su-yin, et al. The Value of the Changing Tongue in Diagnosing Duodenal Perforation. Zhejiang Journal of TCM, 1993 (5): 235-236

43. Ding Cheng-hua, et al. Study on Assiociations between the Appearance of the Tongue and Endoscopic Images in Gastroesophageal Reflux Disease and Infection by H. pylori. Journal of Jiangxi Traditional Chinese Medicine, 2006, 2 (2): 17-19

44. Yang Shu-hui, et al. Research on the Laws of the Appearance of the Tongue and Pulse in Reflux Gastritis. Journal of Hebei Medicine, 2004, 10 (1): 67-69

45. Lin Xiu-ping, Clinical Research on Tongue Diagnosis of Precancerous Lesions in Atrophic Gastritis. Journal of the Shandong University of Traditional Chinese Medicine, 2005, 29 (3): 207-210

46. Yang Yi-fang. Exploration of Tongue Diagnosis Signs in Appendicitis. Journal of TCM Combined with Western Medicine, 1984, (7): 398

47. Wang Su-yin, et al. Tongue Analysis in 489 Patients with Acute Appendicitis. Zhejiang Journal of TCM, 1999, (9): 396

48. Yuan Yi-hong. Preliminary Discussion of the Relationship between the Appearance of the Tongue and Liver Function in Viral Hepatitis. Journal of Jiangsu Traditional Chinese Medicine, 2003, 24 (1): 12

49. Zhang Chi-zhi. Histopathological Observations and the Appearance of the Tongue in Chronic Hepatitis B. China Journal of TCM, 1997, 12 (3): 44

50. Luo Qun. The Relationship between Changes in the Appearance of the Tongue in Patients with Chronic Hepatitis B and Changes in Liver Pathology. Journal of the Zhejiang College of TCM, 1996, 20 (5): 29

51. Xia Jun-qun. Hepatitis B and Observation of the Appearance of the Tongue in 295 Asymptomatic Carriers of the Virus. Liaoning Journal of TCM, 1995, 22 (7): 310-311

52. Zhao Lan-wen. Preliminary Exploration of the Rules of Tongue Diagnosis in the Diagnosis and Treatment of Hepatitis B. Hebei Journal of TCM, 1999, 21 (5): 190

53. Li Nai-Min. Encyclopedia of Chinese Tongue Diagnosis. Beijing: Academy Press, 1994, 1000-1039

54. Li Wei-lin, et al. Analysis of the Relationship between the Appearance of the Tongue

the Prognosis in 35 Patients with Chronic Hepatitis B. Journal of the Modern Integration of Traditional Chinese and Western Medicine, 2002, 11 (1): 28-29

55. He Ling, et al. Discussion of the Laws of Tongue Diagnosis in 208 Patients with Chronic Hepatitis B (moderate). Journal of Sichuan Traditional Chinese Medicine, 2004, 22 (11): 9-10

56. Sun Cheng-qing. Observation of the Appearance of the Tongue in 63 Patients with Hepatic Cirrhosis. Journal of Suzhou University (medical version), 2003, 23 (6): 657

57. Li Feng-chen, et al. The Application of Tongue Diagnosis in Cirrhosis of the Liver. Journal of Traditional Chinese Medicine, 2001, 29 (4): 60-61

58. Tong Guo-quan, et al. Discoveries in the Special Features of Tongue Diagnosis in Primary Hepatocarcinoma-Gan Ying Xian. Fujian Medical Journal, 1962, (6): 7-8

59. Huang Rong-zhang, et al. Analysis of the Appearance of the Tongue in 29 Patients with Hepatocarcinoma. Fujian Medical Journal, 2005, 27 (2): 108

60. Wang Kai-bo. Clinical Research on Changes in the Appearance of the Tongue in Patients with Primary Hepatocarcinoma with Bleeding Complications. Research in Traditional Chinese Medicine, 2002, 18 (3): 14

61. Ling Zhong-guang. Clinical Analysis and Pathomechanism, and Preliminary Exploration of Treatment in 69 Acute Cases of Cholecystitis. Journal of TCM, 1964, (3): 1-4

62. Du Jia-he. Dynamic Observation of the Appearance of the Tongue in 137 Patients with Kidney Disease. Medical Journal of Basic TCM, 2002, 8 (8): 39-40

63. Song Jing-hai. Tongue Diagnosis Research on Chronic Renal Failure. Tianjin Journal of TCM, 1992, (6): 34-36

64. Wang Yi-qin, et al. Quantitive Analysis of the Appearance of the Tongue in Different Syndromes in Patients with Chronic Renal Failure. Journal of the Shanghai University of Traditional Chinese Medicine, 2002, 16 (4): 38-40

65. Li Can-dong. Developments in Chinese Medical Tongue Diagnosis and Endocrine Research. Fujian Journal of TCM, 2001, 11 (2): 58-60

66. Tian Zhi-gao. The Guiding Significance of Tongue Diagnosis to Syndrome Differentiation in Diabetes. Beijing Journal of TCM, 1997, (2): 9

67. Zhou Jiang-yang. Blood Stasis in the Sublingual Vessels and Diabetes. Zhejiang Journal of TCM, 2000, 35 (2): 88

INDEX

图书在版编目（CIP）数据

中医舌诊图谱（英文）/丁成华　孙晓刚
主编．—北京：人民卫生出版社，2008.3
ISBN 978-7-117-09960-8

Ⅰ. 中⋯　Ⅱ. ①丁⋯ ②孙⋯　Ⅲ. 舌诊－图谱
Ⅳ. R241.25-64

中国版本图书馆CIP数据核字（2008）第024424号

中医舌诊图谱（英文）

主　　编：丁成华　孙晓刚
出版发行：人民卫生出版社（中继线 +8610-6761-6688）
地　　址：中国北京市丰台区方庄芳群园三区 3 号楼
邮　　编：100078
网　　址：http://www.pmph.com
E - mail：pmph@pmph.com
发　　行：pmphsales@gmail.com
购书热线：+8610-6769-1034（电话及传真）
开　　本：787×1092　1/16
版　　次：2008 年 4 月第 1 版　2008 年 4 月第 1 版第 1 次印刷
标准书号：ISBN 978-7-117-09960-8/R·9961